BEYOND ALL
CONTROVERSY

To Renee:

May you be blessed
and inspired as you
read & pray.

In the Majesty of Christ,

Joe Christopher

BEYOND ALL CONTROVERSY

Biblical (End-time) Prophecy
A Simplified Version

James Christopher Jackson

Pleasant Word
A Division of WINEPRESS PUBLISHING

Unless otherwise noted, all Scriptures are taken from the Holy Bible, New International Version, Copyright © 1973, 1978, 1984 by the International Bible Society. Used by permission of Zondervan Publishing House. The "NIV" and "New International Version" trademarks are registered in the United States Patent and Trademark Office by International Bible Society.

Scripture references marked KJV are taken from the King James Version of the Bible.

Scripture references marked NASB are taken from the New American Standard Bible, © 1960, 1963, 1968, 1971, 1972, 1973, 1975, 1977 by The Lockman Foundation. Used by permission.

ISBN 1-4141-0429-4
Library of Congress Catalog Card Number: 2005902673

DEDICATION

To my father, whose zeal for the truth was an inspirational revolution!

To my grandmother, the First Lady of Faith, whose endless encouragement has been a bedrock of power!

TABLE OF CONTENTS

ACKNOWLEDGEMENTS OF THANKS

I stand on the shoulders of biblical giants in prophecy. I can only be obedient.

To the Reverend Billy Graham for your faithful obedience to the call of Christ and powerful yet gentle leading of a twelve-year-old in the sinner's prayer.

To Dr. Joseph Stowell of Moody for your transparent and practical sermons of faith.

To Reverend Dr. Marvin McMickle for your challenging and inspiring sermons of action.

To Pastor C. J. Matthews for your insistence upon and recognition of the anointing.

To Pastor Benjamin Garrison, the pastoral model of shepherding and tending to the flock—a father to all in need.

To Pastors Paul and Bonnie Delp, co-laborers in the ministry. There are no words to express our friendship. It's been glorious!

To my mother for providing us with the best education possible.

To my wife for her patience. (Smile)

To all my friends from church, particularly Joyce, Maria, Claudia, Brenda Turner, Brother Brown, Mother Holland, and Sister McMickle.

To my dear sisters and brothers in Christ from Gilead Assembly: Linda, Terry, Joann, Millie, Cindy, Connie, and Marty for allowing me the privilege of ministering to you and for all the wonderful fellowship.

To my trusted Bible study friends who have allowed me to teach over the years: Erik, Megan, Matthew and Katarina, Kevin, Laura Davidson, Ted and Monica, Mark and Mary Madeja, Mark Call, and Scott Gilliam.

To my old colleagues who challenged and inspired me to dig deep in the Word: Ken and Karen Kline, Joyce, Clare DiFranco and Joe, and Bobby and Terri Clarahan.

To Florence Karos and Paige Navratil, whose appreciation of the knowledge of the Word was always a gift of encouragement.

To Rosie and John Korfant for your endless encouragement and friendship.

To Kathy Kuhn and Thomas Martin for your faithful recognition and acknowledgment of the anointing.

To Charlotte Mazzu, Joe Gerald, and Mark Mazzu for allowing me to be part of a wonderful family at First Assembly during my college years.

To my wonderful friends at Rainbow for always allowing me to fellowship and hangout.

To Bob and Bobbie Palmerio and Nancy Tintera for your open door of hospitality and friendship.

To Greg Gainer and Joanie, Jason, Jodie, Kyle, Anna, and Brian for choosing and assisting me in leading an Intervarsity chapter at Kent; and Heather, Mike, Aaron, and Christina for our continual friendship.

To my Elletians, who were a source of great enthusiasm: Sarah G., Brian P. and Gentry, Ariana, John P., Luke, Kevin, Erik J., Doug H., Angela Beaty, Jackie Regis, Anthony Douglas, and Ben.

To Tracy Butler-Ebner, whose patience and word-processing expertise were invaluable.

INTRODUCTION

What is to become of the Church? What is to become of America? Is the world going to end? If the world is going to end, how will it end? Will there ever be peace in the Middle East? What's to become of Western Europe? What is going to happen to Russia?

Where is America in prophecy? Where is Europe? Where is Russia? Is this the end of the American presidency? Or will America cease to be a superpower? Why should we keep our eyes on China? Will China be the only nation to withstand a worldwide depression? Where is China's place in prophecy? What was God's original intention for man? What is the nature of God's character?

The answers to many of these questions are in the Bible, God's only blueprint for eternity. The Bible, God's Word, is one-third prophecy, one-third history, and one-third doctrine and teaching. It has held its own as an international best seller, adorning every home and hotel room.

It is the beginning of the end, or in the words of one of the world's most famous laureates, "It was the best of times. It was the worst of times" (Charles Dickens).

The computer, the car, the television, and the airplane have pushed man to the edge of invincibility; yet war, terrorist bombings, school shootings, ethnic cleansing, and deadly epidemics have cautioned him to prepare for the worst. Never before has man possessed the arsenals to destroy himself and all creation. Never before has the possibility of such force falling into the hands of the irresponsible, deranged, and manic been so probable.

I will begin with a letter that I wrote to a dear friend of our family shortly after the September 11, 2001, terrorist attack:

Dear Mrs. Riche,

You are one of the dearest people we know, and I felt led to share this with you.

There is a minister by the name of David Wilkerson, who is pastor and founder of the Times Square Church at Fifty-first and Broadway and who had a vision of devastation in New York some ten years ago. I remember this because I used to attend the church, and he would warn of this in his newsletters. I would not have dwelled so much on this if it had not (also) happened to me.

Some fifteen years ago, I was fasting and praying on a morning when my uncle was driving me in to work at Northstar Bank of Commerce on Forty-second Street in Manhattan. As I was sitting there on the passenger side of the car, riding down Forty-second Street, I "saw" the buildings coming down on top of the cabs and cars and people screaming and running. I was pinching myself because I was awake, and I didn't say a word at the moment because he (my uncle) would have thought that I was crazy. I later warned everyone in my family about New York. When the World Trade attack occurred and the buildings came down, my mother said, "You saw it, James." My grandmother said, "You predicted it," but that was not what I saw (because) I was on Forty-second Street when I had my vision.

Well, this Pastor David Wilkerson of the Times Square Church said that people have been asking him was this the vision that he had seen. He said, "No, the vision that I saw was much worse." He said he saw "a thousand fires burning at one time all over New York and the fire department was at its wits end as to how to put them out." (My sister had this same dream; she called me terrified one morning. She said that [in the dream] she had driven into Brooklyn looking for my grandmother and there was fire everywhere.)

I am only sharing this because of how close you are to us—not to alarm you or frighten you but to alert you, as I have my family. (May the Lord bless you!)

Always in the majestic love of Christ,
James

CHAPTER 1

THE TIME OF THE END AND
THE PROPHET DANIEL

Those that are wise will shine like the brightness of the heavens and they that lead many to righteousness like the stars forever and ever.

—Daniel 12:3

This is the standard that God told the prophet Daniel He will use at the end of time. It is part of the dual standard that God will use to judge the Hebrew people and all people who have ever lived. (Daniel's book has been noted to be a key book for the end times.)

First, deliverance was promised to all Hebrew people whose names are found written in "the book" (Daniel 12:1). In Revelation 21:27, the apostle John calls the book by name: "The Lamb's Book of Life," maintaining that no one whose name is not written in the book may enter God's holy city.

Second, another standard appears in Daniel 12:3: "those that lead many to righteousness." Those seeking stardom, look no further. God's "Hall of Fame" and "Sunset Boulevard" are reserved for those who teach "righteousness," a foreign word in today's vocabulary.

Politically, you're called right wing for ever mentioning it. Morally, you're called puritanical for ever voicing the thought. Yet the word "righteousness" appears as a standard throughout the Old and New Testament, and if you don't tamper with its meaning or seek to reinterpret it as modern relativist theology has, you will find that it makes sense and may very well be the cure for the majority of today's societal ills.

Daniel was also told in Daniel 12:4 that his book would be a coveted book in the End Times. That people will be running back and forth to get the latest story, and knowledge in general will be increased. And we thought the Internet and the super information highway was a twentieth-century novelty idea. Ha! Daniel saw it coming 2500 years ago via divine revelation.

Also of great significance, Daniel sees a time of trouble for the children of Israel that is unrivaled in history. Daniel 12:1 states:

> And at that time shall Michael stand up, the great prince which standeth for the children of thy people: and there shall be a time of trouble, such as never was since there was a nation even to that same time: and at that time thy people shall be delivered, every one that shall be found written in the book.

Regarding the specific time of the end of the world, or the Second Coming of Christ, Jesus said, "No man knows the day nor the hour, not even the angels in heaven but my Father only" (Matthew 24:36). Jesus, at that moment, went as far as to say that He didn't know. However, He went on to say that you will know when it's coming or how near it is by the succession of things occurring. You will know the "season" (Matthew 24:32–33; Luke 21:29–31).

Just like we know when summer is approaching, when we see all "these things" coming on the earth, we will know that it's time. He also mentions that an entire generation will be locked into this prophecy. The people or persons alive during this age will see its fulfillment. (Ironically, summer is hot, and the heat can be intense, as is the world situation presently.) In Matthew 24:32–34, Jesus states:

> "Now learn a parable of the fig tree; When his branch is yet tender and putteth forth leaves, ye know that summer is near: So likewise ye, when ye shall see all these things, know that it is near, even at the doors. Verily I say unto you, This generation shall not pass till all these things be fulfilled. Heaven and earth shall pass away, but my words shall not pass away."

Luke's gospel records the Lord Jesus giving us a sign that begins the season. Jesus uses the sign of the Gentiles being in control of Jerusalem and then relinquishing control as a marker on the prophetic timeline. (Remember, all biblical prophecy is centered around Jerusalem and the nation of Israel.)

> "And Jerusalem shall be trodden down of the Gentiles until the time of the Gentiles be fulfilled."
> —Luke 21:24

This prophetic marker is very significant, because it coincides with the prophecy of Daniel, the prophet whom Jesus quotes in Matthew

24:15. Daniel goes further than any other prophet by giving us a year or time span to mark the fulfillment of the Gentile reign over Jerusalem.

The times of the Gentiles was fulfilled in 1967 when Jerusalem was captured and again became the capital of Israel under Jewish control (this is a pivotal year in biblical prophecy), two thousand and three hundred years after Alexander the Great conquered the world in 334 B.C., as according to Daniel's prophecy (Daniel 8:14). All historians know that "the he goat and/or the King of Grecia" is Alexander the Great, who is replaced by his four (4) generals (four notable ones) (Daniel 8:8) and/or four kingdoms (Daniel 8:22). (In Daniel's prophecy, days are synonymous for years. Remember, Daniel is prophesying in 553 B.C. None of these events has occurred yet. He is recording the dreams and visions that God is giving him.) Daniel 8:13–14 tells us:

> Then I heard one saint speaking, and another saint said unto that certain saint which spoke, "How long shall be the vision concerning the daily sacrifice, and the transgression of desolation, to give both the sanctuary and the host to be trodden under foot?" And he said unto me, "Unto two thousand and three hundred days; then shall the sanctuary be cleansed."

In fact, this prophecy addresses the length of time that the sanctuary will be desolate and trodden under foot by those who don't know its sacredness (Daniel 8:13–14). Daniel overhears one spirit, or holy one, in Heaven, giving the time span of two thousand three hundred years (2,300 years) (Daniel 8:14). Now, do the math: subtract 334 B.C. from 2300 and you get 1966 A.D. (Actually, 1 B.C. to 1 A.D. is short a year because our calendar does not start from nothing, or zero.) That would make 1966, 1967, the exact year that Jerusalem is recaptured as the Jewish capital. (Note: A thousand years is one day with the Lord [2 Peter 3:8; Psalms 90:4].)

Luke 21:24 is parallel to Daniel 8:13–14 in that Luke describes those doing the trodding as Gentiles. Luke prophesies that the times of the Gentiles will be fulfilled when Jerusalem is no longer trodden by them. In 1967, Jerusalem was returned to the Jewish kingdom of Israel in what we know of as the Six Day War. This has some significant consequences for the Gentile world and their domination, as we will see later. (Remember, God created man on the sixth day, and the seventh day He rested [Genesis 1:31–2:3]. Prophetic scholars believe that the earth is culminating in man's six-thousand-year reign, and the beginning of the seven thousandth year will usher in God's millennial reign, or a thousand years of peace on earth [Revelation 20:1–6; Isaiah 2:1–22]. Hence, God's seventh day of rest for all mankind living on earth begins with His millennial rule beginning after the sixth day [or the six thousand years] of man reigning on earth.)

As far as what hour the Church is currently in, let me share a little jewel that I uncovered regarding the timing. World War I ended on the eleventh hour of the eleventh day of the eleventh month, 1918. It was not planned. Check your history books. It was pure coincidence, or was God sending us a message that the world was in its eleventh hour? (Remember the Bridegroom, the Lord, comes at midnight [see Matthew 25].) Jerusalem is surrounded by armies. The time of the Gentiles is fulfilled. In 1967 Jerusalem returned to the Jews. Israel now has the atomic bomb.

Americans have trusted in the market. They have trusted in real estate and government and their pension. The only real stability is in God—faith in God.

The Two Cousins: Arabs and Jews

Isaac and Ishmael were the sons of Abraham, having the same father but different mothers: Sarah and Hagar, respectively. Their children (the children of the two brothers) are cousins: the Arabs and the Jews. And Jesus holds the key to their getting along: forgiveness. In the flesh, they'll never get along.

Prophecy concerning Ishmael: His hand will be against everyone (Genesis 16:12). Isaac, called in the flesh rather than in the spirit, cannot understand the ways of God. But Jesus' very nature resolves all that. He is the Prince of Peace. He came to reteach man how to live. He said, "Love your enemies…pray for them" (see Matthew 5:43–48). All prophecy is funneled through the cross.

Regarding Ishmael, the Arab link to the patriarch, Abraham, the Scriptures record:

> "And he will be a wild man; his hand will be against every man, and every man's hand against him; and he shall dwell in the presence of all his brethren."
>
> —Gen. 16:12

His hand will be against everyone. This is the prophecy regarding the Arab race, the descendants of Ishmael (after the flesh). Only the cross of Christ can alter it. The September 11, 2001, attack on the World Trade Center in New York with eighty-four nationalities represented seems to make this prophecy a reality. Also, Arabs as a group congregate among themselves, forming whole nations. Also worth noting, in the July 22, 2002, *Newsweek* article, the "Fire that won't Die Out," the Saudi Intelligence Agency produced a confidential poll of men between twenty-five and forty-one, revealing that "[n]inety-five percent said they approved of Osama bin Laden's cause. As one high-ranking Saudi said, 'Fortunately, this is not a democracy.'" Even so, it is frightening that 95 percent of any population could align themselves with someone so devilish.

Remember, all curses die at the cross and all prophecies must be channeled through the cross (Galatians 3:13). "Christ has redeemed us from the curse of the law, being made a curse for us: for it is written, cursed is everyone that hangeth on a tree: That the blessings of Abraham might come on the Gentiles through Jesus Christ; that we might receive the promise of the Spirit through faith" (Galatians 3:13–14).

Curses, prophecies, and judgments are extinguished, modified, and changed once a person surrenders his or her life to Christ. It does not mean that they might not pay for murder in this life, but "true forgiveness," which is foreign to Judaism and Islam (hence, the bedrock, or origin, of the Christian faith and the solution to the Mid-east crisis), can only be found in the person of Jesus Christ who forgave all for His death ("Father, forgive them, for they know not what they do" [Luke 23:34]). With one breath, Jesus could have called twelve legions of angels to defend Himself (Matthew 26:53), but He took the judgment of the world upon Himself to allow His Holy Father to grant us access into Heaven (John 3:16–17).

> "For God so loved the world, that He gave His only begotten Son, that whosoever believeth in Him should not perish, but have everlasting life. For God sent not His Son into the world to condemn the world but that the world through Him might be saved."
>
> —John 3:16–17

With regard to Isaac, Abraham and Sarah's only son between them, God entrusted the covenant to him via his miraculous birth and the blood covenant seal of circumcision (Genesis 17:10–11). God was distinctly clear as to which of Abraham's children would prophetically fulfill the everlasting covenant.

> And God said unto Abraham, "As for Sarai thy wife, thou shalt not call her name Sarai, but Sarah shall her name be. And I will bless

her, and give thee a son also of her: yea, I will bless her, and she shall be a mother of nations; kings of people shall be of her." Then Abraham fell upon his face, and laughed and said in his heart, "Shall a child be born unto him that is an hundred years old? And shall Sarah, that is ninety years old, bear?" And Abraham said unto God, "O that Ishmael might live before thee!" And God said, "Sarah thy wife shall bear thee a son indeed; and thou shalt call his name Isaac: and I will establish my covenant with him for an everlasting covenant, and with his seed after him! And as for Ishmael, I have heard thee: Behold, I have blessed him and will make him fruitful, and will multiply him exceedingly; twelve princes shall he beget, and I will make him a great nation. But my covenant will I establish with Isaac."

—Gen. 17:15–21

The Day of the Lord

The day of the Lord is an ominous day for the world. It reads like nuclear disaster (2 Peter 3:7–12; Malachi 4:1–3; Joel 2:1–3, 11–12):

But the day of the Lord will come as a thief in the night: in the which the heavens shall pass away with a great noise, and the elements shall melt with fervent heat, the earth also and the works that are therein shall be burned up. Seeing then that all these things shall be dissolved, what manner of persons ought ye to be in all holy conversation and godliness. Looking for and hasting unto the coming of the day of God, wherein the heavens being on fire shall be dissolved, and the elements shall melt with fervent heat?

—2 Pet. 3:10–12

"For, behold, the day cometh, that shall burn as an oven; and all the proud, yea, and all that do wickedly, shall be stubble; and the day that cometh shall burn them up," saith the LORD of hosts, "that it shall leave them neither root nor branch. But unto you that fear my name shall the Sun of righteousness arise with healing in his wings; and ye shall go forth, and grow up as calves of the stall."

—Mal. 4:1–2

Blow ye the trumpet in Zion, and sound an alarm in my holy mountain: let all the inhabitants of the land tremble: for the day of the LORD cometh, for it is nigh at hand; A day of darkness and of gloominess, a day of clouds and of thick darkness, as the morning spread upon the mountains: a great people and a strong; there hath not been ever the like, neither shall be any more after it, even to the years of many generations. A fire devoureth before them; and behind them a flame burneth: the land is as the garden of Eden before them, and behind them a desolate wilderness; yea, and nothing shall escape them.

—Joel 2:1–3

Initially, Old Testament prophets referred to it as a day of judgment on the Gentiles, or non-Jewish, enemies. This was pre-Amos' prophetic age. As Israel began to resemble the world, the prophets began to refer to the day as a day of judgment on all the wickedness and unrighteousness of mankind (Wickliffe, 1356). God has proven that He can judge the wicked and spare the righteous from judgment (i.e., Noah, Lot, and the Israelites in Egypt). Just as Shadrach, Meshach, and Abednego miraculously escaped the fiery furnace in Daniel chapter three, God promises to judge the wicked and spare the righteous from judgment (2 Peter 2:9–10).

The day of the Lord has been said to follow the Antichrist and the great apostasy, or the hour of temptation, which shall try the whole world (i.e., the Tribulation period) (2 Thessalonians 2:1–12). But God has again promised His church, the church of Philadelphia (or "the church of brotherly love" that kept His word and did not deny His name), that He would keep them from the hour of temptation that shall try the whole world (Revelation 3:7–13).

"Now we beseech you, brethren, by the coming of our Lord Jesus Christ, and by our gathering together unto him, that you be not soon shaken in mind, or be troubled, neither by spirit, nor by word, nor by letter as from us, as that the day of Christ is at hand. Let no man deceive you by any means: for that day shall not come, except there come a falling away first, and that man of sin be revealed, the son of perdition; who opposeth and exalteth himself above all that is called God, or that is worshipped; so that he as God sitteth in the temple of God, shewing himself that he is God. Remember ye not, that, when I was yet with you, I told you these things? And now ye

know what withholdeth that he might be revealed in his time. For the mystery of iniquity
doth already work: only he who now letteth
will let, until he be taken out of the way.
And then shall that Wicked (Lawless one) be
revealed, whom the Lord shall consume with
the spirit of his mouth, and shall destroy with
the brightness of His coming: even him whose
coming is after the working of Satan with
all power and signs and lying wonders, and
with all deceivableness of unrighteousness
in them that perish; because they received
not the love of the truth, that they might
be saved. And for this cause God shall send
them strong delusion, that they should believe a lie: that they all might be damned who
believed not the truth, but had pleasure in
unrighteousness."

—2 Thess. 2:1–12

This passage is about the Antichrist, who will
come and demand that all the people of the earth
worship him and receive the mark of the beast
(which is the number 666) on their hand and/or
forehead for the purpose of buying or trading.
This is spelled out very clearly in Revelation
chapter thirteen. (Note: the Lord will destroy

him, the Antichrist, with the word of His mouth at the "brightness of His coming.")

The Lord encourages the church that they have nothing to worry about if they keep His word and not deny His name:

And to the angel of the church in Philadelphia write: These things saith he that is holy, he that is true, he that hath the key of David, he that openeth, and no man shutteth; and shutteth, and no man openeth; I know thy works: behold, I have set before thee an open door, and no man can shut it: for thou hast a little strength, and has kept my word, and hast not denied my name. Behold, I will make them of the synagogue of Satan, which say they are Jews, and are not, but do lie; behold, I will make them to come and worship before thy feet, and to know that I have loved thee. Because thou hast kept the word of my patience, I also will keep thee from the hour of temptation, which shall come upon all the world, to try them that dwell upon the earth. Behold, I come quickly: hold that fast which thou hast, that no man take thy crown. Him that overcometh will I make a pillar in the temple of my God, and he shall go no more out: and I will write upon him the name of my God, and the name of the city of my God, which is new Jerusalem, which cometh down out of heaven from my God: and I will write upon him my new name. He that hath an ear, let him hear what the Spirit saith unto the churches."

—Rev. 3:7–13

God's Prophetic Calendar

"And this Gospel of the Kingdom shall be preached in all the world for a witness to all nations, and then the end shall come."

—Matt. 24:14
—Jesus

"But thou, O Daniel, shut up the words, and seal the book, even to the time of the end: many shall run to and fro (mass transportation and travel), and knowledge ("super information highway") shall be increased."

—Dan. 12:4, Dan. 10:5–9,
Rev. 1:8–18
—the Lord

"Now, I am come to make thee understand what shall befall thy people (the children of Israel) in the latter days: for yet the vision is for many days."

—Dan. 10:14
—the Lord

And the seventh angel poured out his vial into the air; and there came a great voice out of the temple of heaven, from the throne, saying, "It is done." And there were voices, and thunders, and lightnings; and there was a great earthquake, such as was not since men were upon the earth, so mighty an earthquake and so great. And the great city (Jerusalem) was divided into three parts, and the cities of the nations fell: and great Babylon came in remembrance before God, to give unto her the cup of the wine of the fierceness of His wrath. And every island fled away, and the mountains were not found.

—Rev. 16:17–20

"And it shall come to pass afterward (in the last days), that I will pour out my spirit upon all flesh and your sons and daughters will prophesy and your young men will see visions and your old men will dream dreams, even on my maidservant and manservant will I pour out my spirit."

—Joel 2:28–29

CHAPTER 2

QUESTIONS AND ANSWERS

According to the Scriptures, Where Is Jesus?

J esus is sitting at the right hand of God until all His enemies are conquered, the last enemy being death. Then Jesus will take off His crown and bow before God the Father, that God may be God all in all (Ephesians 1:19–23; 1 Corinthians 15:20–28; see also Hebrews 8:1 and 12:2).

And what is the exceeding greatness of his power to us-ward who believe, according to the working of his mighty power, which he wrought in Christ, when he raised him from the dead, and set him at his own right hand in heavenly places, Far above all principality, and power, and might, and dominion, and every name that is named, not only in this world, but also in that which is to come: And has put all things under his feet and gave him to be the head over all things to the church, which is his body, the fullness of him that filleth all in all.

—Eph. 1:19–23

Then cometh the end, when he shall have put down all rule and all authority and power, For he must reign, till he has put all enemies under his feet. The last enemy that shall be destroyed is death.... And when all things shall be subdued unto him, then shall the Son also himself be subject unto him that put all things under him, that God may be all in all.

—1 Cor. 15:24–28

Where Is the United States in Prophecy?

There are four possibilities for the United States in prophecy:

1. *The US is just one of the Gentile nations and has no specific reference in prophecy. She is destroyed by cataclysm, or disaster, and experiences the fate of the other Gentile nations not playing a major end-time role. (I feel that this view is lacking, given America's role in the formation and establishment of modern-day Israel and her present status as a world power.)*

2. *The US becomes part of the Antichrist's system. If America has Star Wars, a strategic arms defense system (Revelation 13), no nation can challenge her. "Who is like the beast? Who can make war with her?" (Only time will tell if this is the road that America chooses to travel. Remember, a nation has a will, just like an individual; however, all are subject to the will of God and prayer.)*

3. *America is the last haven for Israel and the Church. She is the place in the "wilderness" prepared by God, where*

Israel and the Church is fed, nourished, protected, and preserved from the face of the serpent, the devil for a period of time, times, and half a time, as described in Revelation 12:5–6 and 13–14. (There is great evidence and support for this view, given the freedoms of religion, of speech, of the press, of assembly, and of petition built into our constitution, making this land a haven for all who love God and desire "life, liberty, and the pursuit of happiness.")

4. *As I get "Holy Ghost chills," America is Israel replanted supernaturally. She is also represented by the eagle in Ezekiel, chapter seventeen. If you know your Bible, what I am about to share will be crystal clear to your understanding. As I kept researching in the Spirit for America in prophecy, the word that kept coming to me was: "Follow the eagle." The eagle is America's great symbol of freedom and superiority—the bird that is able to soar far above all the predators and pitfalls of earth.*

   I was led to Ezekiel, chapter seventeen. Exegetically, this passage speaks of Babylon and Israel in the natural, but the Old Testament Scriptures have a way of foreshadowing what is to come in the future via the Holy Spirit. For example, Abraham offered up his only son with Sarah as a sacrifice, just like God the Father offered up His only begotten son, Jesus. Jacob had twelve sons that became the foundational pillars for the nation of Israel, just like Jesus had twelve apostles that became the foundational pillars for the Church. The deliverer, Moses, was spared the death of a king's edict as his parents sought to hide him, just like Jesus, whose name means "deliverer," was spared the death of a king's edict as his parents sought to hide Him in Egypt. If the evidence of Old Testament foreshadowing and type is not convincing enough, consider one more jewel: Moses stood in between Israel and God's wrath in the wilderness, just like Jesus stands in between all the world/humanity and God's wrath in the wilderness of life. (See Exodus 32:7–14; John 3:16–21.)

Now, the purpose of this background knowledge is to show the power of the Old Testament to foreshadow future events. This brings us back to our pas-

sage in Ezekiel 17:3–6. This passage speaks of the eagle transplanting the House of Israel into a "land of traffic" and a "city of merchants." Now we know the passage is referring to Babylon in the natural because it told us. We know in history that Babylon conquered Israel and placed the king, princes, and leadership in exile. However, just like Babylon was described as a city of merchants and a land of traffic, New York, which boasts the largest concentration of Jewish people in America, is also a city of merchants in a land of traffic. Many theologians refer to New York as spiritual Babylon. (Those of you who've been there can see this.)

Now to prevent our exegetical Bible-thumpers from having a conniption over superimposing New York onto Babylon, this passage has another eagle in Ezekiel 17:7 and 17:8. The great eagle becomes the caretaker of the House of Israel. Here, the great eagle is not doing any transplanting, but the House of Israel has reached out to the great eagle for nurturing and nourishment. The House of Israel is described as planted in "good soil by great waters."

Now, if this doesn't describe America, I don't know what does. Our symbol is the great eagle. It is on our money and our presidential seal. The United States has taken it upon itself to be the caretaker and nurturer of the House of Israel in the Middle East. The American Jews who call America home know of its "great waters," or great lakes, that nurture and nourish everything here. "Great waters" could also represent the great ocean barriers that isolate America: the Atlantic and Pacific Oceans. Ironically, if you look at the passage as a time marker, 17:7 and 17:8 as 1770 and 1780, you will note that this is where the other great eagle first gets mentioned and when the United States of America becomes a nation.

Ironically, Osama Bin Laden released a press message that he wanted to die a martyr in the heart of the eagle. Israel is the heart of the eagle in the Middle East. Politically, it is the American presence in the Middle East. Spiritually, Israel is the land of the Bible: it is the birthplace *of Christ, the place of His crucifixion and death, and the place of His glorious resurrection. All the world of Christendom flocks to the birth, death, and resurrection sites of Christ. All of our hymns and songs reference Israel.*

Some theologians believe that America is Israel transplanted in the wilderness. The evidence is startling, for the history of Israel and America mirror one another. In its conception, Israel had thirteen tribes (twelve plus Levi, "the priestly tribe"); America began with thirteen colonies. Israel split into two nations (Israel and Judah) when the king (Rehoboam) insisted on overtaxing the people; America split from Great Britain when the king (George III) insisted on overtaxing the people without representation. Even our thirteenth colony, Rhode Island, founded by the separatist, Roger Williams, mirrors the tribe of Levi (the separated priestly tribe). Williams, naming the capital Providence, which means "God," believed that the Church should be separate from the state. (Government officials should stick to government and leave church matters alone.) Also, Wil-

liams believed that the land should be purchased from the Indians as Abraham purchased the land of Canaan and as King David purchased the land for the building of the Temple. Even America's unwritten allegiance to the royal family of England mirrors Israel's allegiance to the House of Judah, the royal house of David. (See "British Monarchy" later in this chapter.)

What Is the Significance of Babylon?

Now, we know that the passage in Ezekiel 17 is about Babylon, and this passage is a message about Babylon. The Lord God is saying that He will use Babylon to judge Israel for its trespasses and sins (Ezekiel 17:20–21). Babylon's presence signifies judgment, and the east wind reference as having the power to wither the prosperous tree (Ezekiel 17:10). We are spending $1 billion a week to keep our soldiers in modern-day Iraq (Babylon). The enemy there is using our soldiers for target practice, and there seems to be no end to this war on terror and its costs. Could this be America's judgment?

In Revelation, chapters seventeen and eighteen, Babylon represents the apostate Church, doomed to God's judgment for seducing the kings and people of the earth and murdering God's saints. God promises to destroy her in one hour (Revelation 18:10).

What About the Economic Turmoil in Asia and Russia?

Those knowledgeable of history see the danger of parading wealth in front of those who view it as utterly unattainable and themselves stuck in the vise grip of hopeless poverty. You need only say the words *"French Revolution"* and *"Russian Revolution"* to the historian to conjure up images of the wealthy and the nobility being rounded up and executed by the masses. America and Britain's (and that of the free West) saving grace is that they have allowed education and socialism to become the great equalizers to confront hopelessness and despair, as Franklin D. Roosevelt's legacy declares. *The Bible foresaw the economic turmoil that we see in Russia, Asia, Latin America (Venezuela), and in history, long before it was ever actually seen.* It was one based in principle as to the attitude of the rich toward the poor. *Christianity and true philanthropy has spared America the gravest of consequences,* which the Bible declares:

Now listen, you rich people, weep and wail because of the misery that is coming upon you. Your wealth has rotted, and moths have eaten your clothes. Your gold and silver are corroded. Their corrosion will testify against you and eat your flesh like fire. You have hoarded wealth in the last days. Look! The wages you failed to pay the workmen who mowed your fields are crying out against you. The cries of the harvesters have reached the ears of the Lord Almighty. You have lived on earth in luxury and self-indulgence. You have fattened yourselves in the day of slaughter. You have condemned and murdered innocent men, who were not opposing you.

—James 5:1–6

What About All the Fatal Shootings by Children?

I remember a few years ago when there was over 2,100 school shootings (from information published by Dr. James Dobson of Focus on the Family); however, only the most sensational and deadly received any publicity. The Word of God declares:

This know also, that in the last days, perilous times shall come. For men shall be lovers of their own selves, covetous, boasters, proud, blasphemers, disobedient to parents, unthankful, unholy, without natural affection, trucebreakers, false accusers, incontinent, fierce, despisers of those that are good, traitors, heady, highminded, lovers of pleasures more than lovers of God.

—2 Tim. 3:1–4

What About All the Outrageous Weather, Hurricanes, and Flooding?

"And there shall be signs in the sun, and in the moon, and in the stars; and upon the earth distress of nations, with perplexity; the sea and the waves roaring; Men's hearts failing them for fear, and for looking after those things which are coming on the earth: for the powers of heaven shall be shaken."

—Luke 21:25–26

What is "Hot" and "Cold" Love?

Hot love is passionate. Cold love is just that—icy. In the prophetic chapters of Matthew 24 and Luke 17 and 21, Jesus gives us insight into the present state of things at the time of His coming. These chapters answer questions that you would have today.

For instance, why are people so hateful today? Because of sin.

"Because iniquity (sin) shall abound, the love of many shall wax cold."

—Matt. 24:11

In other words, because of the sinful condition of the world, people will stop loving one another.

Noah's Day

Noah's days were the Lord's prophetic marker describing the state of the world at the time of His coming. (Ironically, they just found the Ark a few years ago in the mountains of Turkey.)

"As in the days of Noah, so shall the coming of the Son of Man be. For as in the days that were before the flood, they were eating and drinking, marrying and giving in marriage, until the day that Noah entered the Ark. And they knew not until the flood came and took them all away. So also shall the coming of the Son of Man be."

—Matt. 24:37–39; See Luke 17:26–27

How was it in Noah's day?

And God saw that the wickedness of man was great in the earth, and that every imagination of the thoughts of his heart was only evil continually. And it repented the LORD that he had made man on the earth, and it grieved him to his heart. And the LORD said, I will destroy man whom I have created from the face of the earth; both man and beast, and the creeping thing, and the fowls of the air; for it repented me that I have made them. . . . The earth was also corrupt before God, and the earth was filled with violence. And God looked upon the earth, and, behold, it was corrupt; for all flesh had corrupted his way upon the earth. And God said unto Noah, "The end of all flesh is come before me; for the earth is filled with violence through them; and behold, I will destroy them with the earth."

—Gen. 6:5–7, 11–13

Genesis chapter six tells us that the earth was filled with violence. Hollywood continues to spew out more and more violence as Americans become drunk with depravity. God set out to destroy the human race because of this. God did warn man through Noah, but men were too drunk, or intoxicated, with pleasure to care. This is why I refuse to watch violent movies. Most importantly, the world was so consumed with business that it was clueless to God's judgment on the horizon. Jesus said that it will be the same right before He returns.

Amazingly, Noah's ark was found in the mountains of Turkey just recently. Not surprising—the Kurds of Turkey traditionally call Ararat *Koh-i-Nu* ("Mountain of Noah"). This is a sign, saints, people of God. This is a sign.

How Will the Heavens Announce His Coming?

For the past few years, fireballs have been streaking across the western skies. You will see more of these things.

> "And great earthquakes shall be in divers places, and famines and pestilences; and fearful sights and great signs shall there be from heaven.... And there shall be signs in the sun, and in the moon, and in the stars; and upon the earth distress of nations, with perplexity; the sea and the waves roaring; men's hearts failing them for fear, and for looking after those things which are coming on the earth: for the powers of heaven shall be shaken. And then shall they see the Son of Man coming in a cloud with power and great glory."
> —Luke 21:11, 26–28

See, these astronomical, celestial, and terrestrial signs are to let us know that He is coming. *Jesus is coming back!*

"And when these things begin to come to pass, then look up, and lift up your heads; for your redemption draweth nigh."

—Luke 21:28

Does the Bible Address Nuclear Waste in This Nuclear Age?

Revelation 8:10–11 discusses the falling of a great star, whose name is Wormwood, from Heaven that pollutes one-third of the rivers and fountains of waters. The waters then become "wormwood" and bitter, and many men die from the waters. By no coincidence, the word for "wormwood" in Russian is "Chernobel." Those familiar with current events know that the Chernobel nuclear disaster was one of the greatest nuclear disasters in history, contaminating everything from humans to livestock and causing cancer generationally.

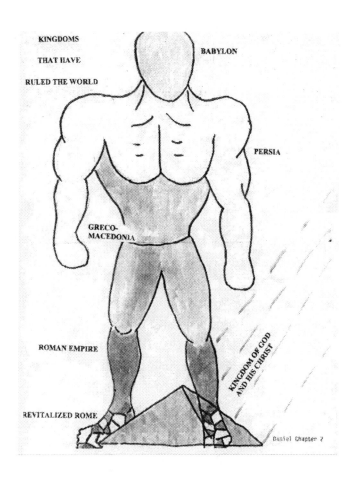

What Does the Bible Say about Europe and the Antichrist?

Europe and the Antichrist to Come

Europe is the seat of the Old Roman Empire, and according to all accounts of biblical prophecy, its drive toward the secular will land it into the hands of the Antichrist. The only question is timing. How soon or how fast will the Antichrist seize the allegiance of the United States of Europe?

According to Bible scholar Jack Van Impe:

Daniel chapter two and chapter seven reveal the kingdoms that have ruled the world. The image that Daniel saw in his dream in chapter two represents five kingdoms that have or will rule the world:

1. Head of gold (the Babylonian Empire 605–539 B.C.)
2. Arms and chest of silver (the Persian Empire 539–330 B.C.)
3. Belly and thighs of brass (Greco-Macedonian Empire 330– 60 B.C.)
4. Legs of iron (the Roman Empire 60 B.C.–A.D. 476)
5. Toes of clay and iron (the Revitalized Roman Empire–present to future)

6. Rock mountain (the kingdom of God and His Christ)

    (Note: The iron and the clay mixtures of the toes represent a kingdom strong and divided—strong militarily, but weak because they're all democracies.)

"The final world power (the Revitalized Roman Empire) will be a confederation of ten western nations out of the Old Roman Empire making up the European Economic Community, or the United States of Europe. One nation will replace three nations and out of that nation will come the Antichrist" (Impe, "Revelation Revealed" Part 3 Video). (See Revelation, chapters thirteen and seventeen, for further reading).

The kingdom of God and His Christ will crush the toes and feet of this image, and all the other kingdoms will come crashing down; and their residue will be swept away by the wind, and the kingdom of God will fill the entire earth.

Historians marvel at Daniel's prophetic accuracy in these dreams, which he had between 603 B.C. and 555 B.C., during the reign of the Babylonian Empire and before the domination of the other empires. Daniel chapter 7 sees these

KINGDOMS THAT HAVE RULED THE WORLD

BABYLON

PERSIA

GRECO-MACEDONIA

ROMAN EMPIRE

Daniel Chapter 7

same kingdoms that have ruled the world in animal form. See image 2.

Bible scholar Dave Breese concurs:

In its final form, [the Revitalized Rome or Present Day Europe] will be both unified and divided, divided into ten kingdoms but unified as a kingdom in and of itself under a great leader. It is that complicated, political entity, the Reconstituted Roman Empire, which will produce, according to the prophet Daniel, the prince that shall come, [the Antichrist]." (Breese, 34).

—See Daniel 7:25 and Daniel 8:23–35

According to Breese,

When the United States of Europe comes to pass, it could quickly become the most powerful political force in the world. A United States of Europe will have a population of 320 million and will instantly possess unified economic strength that is larger than that of the United States. It will therefore have economic, commercial power which will be second to none in the entire world.

—Breese, 18-19

Professor and author J. Dwight Pentecost affirms that "[h]e, [the Antichrist], rises from the Roman Empire, since he is a ruler of the people who destroyed Jerusalem" (Daniel 9:26) (Pentecost, 332). Pentecost gives the most extensive description of the Antichrist:

Scripture has a great deal to say concerning the individual who will appear in the end time as the head of the Gentile powers in their ten kingdom federation. His person and work are presented in Ezekiel 28:1–10; Daniel 7:7–8, 20–26; 8:23–25; 9:26–27; 11:36–45; 2 Thessalonians 2:3–10; Revelation 13:1–10; 17:8–14. A synthesis of the truths in these passages will reveal the following facts concerning his activities: (1) He will appear on the scene in the "latter times" of Israel's history (Dan. 8:23). (2) He will not appear until the day of the Lord has begun (2 Thess.2:2). (3) His manifestation is being hindered by the Restrainer (2 Thess. 2:6–7). (4) This appearance will be preceded by a departure (2 Thess. 2:3), which may be interpreted either as a departure from the faith or a departure of the saints to be with the Lord (2 Thess. 2:1). (5) He is a Gentile. Since he rises from the sea (Rev. 13:1) and since the sea depicts the Gentile nations (Rev. 17:15), he must be of Gentile origin. (6) He rises from the Roman empire, since he is a ruler of the people who destroyed Jerusalem (Dan. 9:26). (7) He is the head of the last form

of Gentile world dominion, for he is like a
leopard, a bear, and a lion (Rev. 13:11). (Cf.
Dan. 7:7–8, 20, 24; Rev. 17:9–11). As such he
is a political leader. The seven heads and ten
horns (Rev. 13:1; 17:12) are federated under
his authority. (8) His influence is worldwide,
for he rules over all nations (Rev. 13:8). This
influence comes through the alliance which
he makes with other nations (Dan. 8:24; Rev.
17:12). (9) He has eliminated three rulers in
his rise to power (Dan 7:8, 24). One of the
kingdoms over which he has authority has
been revived, for one of the heads, representing a kingdom or a king (Rev. 17:10), has
been healed (Rev. 13:3). (10) His rise comes
through his peace program (Dan. 8:25). (11)
He personally is marked by his intelligence
and persuasiveness (Dan. 7:8, 20; 8:23) and
also by his subtlety and craft (Ezek. 28:6),
so that his position over the nations is by
their own consent (Rev. 17:13). (12) He
rules over the nations in his federation with
absolute authority (Dan. 11:36), where he is
depicted as doing his own will. This authority
is manifested through the change in laws and
customs (Dan. 7:25). (13) His chief interest
is in might and power (Dan. 11:38). (14) As
the head of the federated empire, he makes a
seven year covenant with Israel (Dan. 9:27),
which is broken after three and one-half years

(Dan. 9:27). (15) He introduces an idolatrous worship (Dan. 9:27) in which he sets himself up as god (Dan. 11: 36–37; 2 Thess. 2:4; Rev. 13:5). (16) He bears the characterization of a blasphemer because of the assumption of deity (Ezek. 28:2; Dan. 7:25; Rev. 13: 1, 5–6). (17) This one is energized by Satan (Ezek. 28:9–12; Rev. 13:4), receives his authority from him, and is controlled by the pride of the devil (Ezek. 28:2, Dan. 8:25). (18) He is the head of Satan's lawless system (2 Thess. 2:3) and his claim to power and to deity is proved by signs wrought through satanic power (2 Thess. 2: 9–19). (19) He is received as God and as ruler because of the blindness of the people (2 Thess. 2:11). (20) This ruler becomes the great adversary of Israel (Dan. 7:21, 25; 8:24; Rev. 13:7). (21) There will come an alliance against him (Ezek. 28:7; Dan. 11:40, 42) which will contest his authority. (22) In the ensuing conflict, he will gain control over Palestine and adjacent territory (Dan. 11: 42) and will make his headquarters in Jerusalem (Dan. 11:45). (23) This ruler, at the time of his rise to power, is elevated through the instrumentality of the harlot, the corrupt religious system, which consequently seeks to dominate him (Rev. 17:3). (24) This system is destroyed by the ruler so that he may rule unhindered (Rev. 17:16–17). (25)

He becomes the special adversary of the Prince of Princes (Dan. 8:25), His program (2 Thess.2:4; Rev. 17:14), and His people (Dan. 7:21, 25; 8:24; Rev. 13:7). (26) While he continues in power for seven years (Dan. 9:27), his satanic activity is confined to the last half of the tribulation period (Dan. 7:25; 9:27; 11:36; Rev. 13:5). (27) His rule will be terminated by a direct judgment from God (Ezek. 28:6; Dan. 7:22, 26; 8:25; 9:27; 11:45; Rev. 19:19–20). This judgment will take place as he is engaged in a military campaign in Palestine (Ezek. 28:8–9; Rev. 19:19), and he will be cast into the lake of fire (Rev. 19:20; Ezek. 28:10). (28) This judgment will take place at the second advent of Christ (2 Thess. 2:8; Dan. 7:22) and will constitute a manifestation of His Messianic authority (Rev. 11:15). (29) The kingdom over which he ruled will pass to the authority of the Messiah and will become the kingdom of the saints (Dan. 7:27).

The Church has been the only barrier throughout time and history holding back the tide. Some of the greatest reformers and theologians in history have come out of the European church: Thomas Aquinas, Constantine, Martin Luther, John Wickliffe, John Calvin, and John Wesley. It is greatly feared that the Church throughout Europe and the world lacks the integrity to hold back the tide of secularism and hedonism plaguing the world. The Church had always been in stark contrast to the world. Today the compromise and indifference have created a fusion of confusion, where the Church and the world are indistinguishable in terms of behavior and attitude.

From its conception in the womb of a virgin to this modern day, what has distinguished the Church from the world has been "its zeal to holiness." The desire to follow Christ in Word and deed: "Righteousness." It is righteousness in its literal definition not the interpretive definition used by the Church today. The Church today uses the word to mean only the work of Christ and not the actions of men as it was used in time past. It was His righteousness that ended slavery, banned alcohol, and led to every awakening, revival, and reformation that the Church has ever seen. Read your history. It was the Church's zeal for holiness that precipitated these events. Not a holiness born out of legalism but a holiness endued by the Holy Spirit manifesting the attribute that we scarcely talk about: temperance, or self-control.

The Church has failed to hold up God's banner of holiness as the attainable standard. In lust, passion, and appetite, she has refused to deny herself. *The reason why she has no power is because she has neglected the key to the kingdom: "prayer," and in reassessing times of testing and trouble: "fasting."* She has gone about her business being seduced by the world and led by the world rather than being the beacon of light that her Creator fashioned her to be. What shall we do? Start praying and reading the Word. Fast a day or three to purge yourself of sinful, lustful desires, and I guarantee that the Holy Spirit will speak to you. While you fast and pray, read the Word, for the Holy Spirit will never lead you in opposition to the Word. Remember, the Word is God, and before the written Word was the spoken Word spoken to men's hearts.

The Heavens and the Earth Will be Shaken

He said, "Once I shook the earth, but I will not only shake the earth but the heavens also. Meteorites will fall to the earth poisoning the water supply. Only wine and bottled beverages will be safe" (Revelation 8:10–11).

The earthquake of the century will hit California. All the pornography and many wineries and hi-tech conglomerates will sink beneath the Pacific. The date I'm not sure of.

A hurricane, whose root is Jacob, will strike the Caribbean with such force, nothing will ever be the same. The earthquake will trigger it (Luke 21:25–26).

What Will be the Fate of the British Monarchy?

Elizabeth II, queen of the United Kingdom and its province, may be the last monarch to complete her reign. Some years ago, Queen Elizabeth II returned the coronation stone to Scotland, a stone that, for over a thousand years, the monarchs of Europe have been coronated upon. Irish folklore records that an old man, the prophet Jeremiah, brought and placed a stone from his former kingdom beneath the princess, the daughter of the King Zedekiah, king of Judah, as she was wedded into the royal families of England and Scotland. Queen Elizabeth II returned this stone as a goodwill gesture, but its effects will be profound for the monarchy. (I pray Scotland will give it back.)

On *World News Tonight* with Peter Jennings, a clip was shown of the anniversary of the June 2, 1953, coronation of Elizabeth. As it rolled, the Archbishop of Canterbury said, "And thou O Queen doth sit upon the throne of David until Shiloh comes." With these final words, he placed the crown upon her head. I literally fell out of my easy chair, stunned at the revelation. All prophecy and history converged on that Elizabeth II is sitting upon the throne of David until the Messiah, Christ, replaces her. For all you skeptics, go watch the clip and listen to the archbishop's words. (For an in-depth understanding, read the Davidic Covenant with Scripture references: 2 Samuel 7:4–17 and Genesis 49:10. The Davidic Covenant appears in chapter seven of this text.)

The Book of Proverbs in the Holy Bible is the book of sound government for kings. If the stone is returned, Prince William should make certain that he understands the principles of this book and the comfort of the Psalms.

Who Is the Beast of Revelation 13?

> And I stood upon the sand of the sea, and saw a beast rise up out of the sea, having seven heads and ten horns, and upon his horns ten crowns and upon his heads the name of blasphemy. And the beast which I saw was like unto a leopard, and his feet were as the feet of a bear, and his mouth as the mouth of a lion: and the dragon gave him his power, and his seat and great authority.
>
> —Rev. 13:1–2

This beast with ten horns conquers the whole world, blasphemes the name of the Most High God, and makes war with the saints in Revelation 13:1–10. Most scholars and theologians agree that the beast of Revelation 13 is the Roman Empire. It is the fourth kingdom (iron) to rule the entire world as mentioned above (Daniel 2:40). It is the fourth beast called "dreadful and terrible" (Daniel 7:7, also mentioned above and displayed in the chart).

The ten toes of Daniel 2:40–43 and the ten horns of Daniel 7:7–8 are one and the same. They are the ten nations that rise up out of the Old Roman Empire at the end of the world or end of the age of which the Antichrist shall come. It is believed to be the United States of Europe. It is partly strong because of technology and industrialization and partly weak because of democracy and nationalism. As Daniel 2:42–43 records, their individuality will always be apparent.

It is at this time that the God of Heaven will destroy this kingdom and the residue of all the kingdoms that have come before, and He will set up His kingdom—the stone from the mountain that destroys the world systems and becomes a great mountain filling the whole earth (Daniel 2:35, 44–45).

CHAPTER 3

THE CHURCH AT ODDS WITH GOD

The Church has positioned itself to be at odds with our Holy Father and Jesus, His Most Holy Son. In its endeavor to eliminate works from the equation of salvation, it has bludgeoned accountability to death. Then the Church has the nerve to ask what has happened to our degenerate culture and why divorce rates, sexual promiscuity, and teenage rebellion in the Church parallel the world. To put it in layman's terms: *"It's the doctrine, stupid!"*

Go back to your history: It was not sufficient to profess the name of Jesus in order to be a member of the Church. Awakening revivalists, Gilbert Tennent, Jonathan Edwards, and George

Whitefield, "argued for conversion experience validated by a changed life as necessary to church membership" (McDow & Reid, 209–211). The Church stumbles over the changed life because pastors refuse to give up their pet sins. In their attempt to avoid hypocrisy, by their silence on sin they are sending generations to hell devoid of truth and holiness. They have allowed compromise to so flood their souls that they preach sermons devoid of conviction and power.

Without holiness, your Bible collapses. God is a holy God, and without holiness no man will see God (Hebrews 12:14). Repentance brings us into a right relationship with God, but there is a walk of righteousness that God requires even if we imperfectly walk in it. David spoke of this walk in the early Psalms even though he failed miserably later in life. God's standard has not changed. The Lord Jesus tells us to "be perfect as our heavenly Father is perfect; to be holy as He is Holy" (Matthew 5:48; see 1 Peter 1:15–16).

The problem is no one wants to crucify the flesh with its affections and desires as our Lord mandates in Luke 9:23. Crucifixion and self-denial are painful and hard work. Jesus said, "If any man come after me, let him deny himself, take up his cross and follow me."

In the Book of Philippians, the apostle Paul said, touching the law, he was blameless (Philippians 3:6). In 1 Corinthians 6:9-11, the apostle Paul thundered against sin, maintaining that if you do certain acts you will not inherit the kingdom:

> Do you not know that the wicked will not inherit the kingdom of God? Do not be deceived: Neither the sexually immoral nor idolaters nor adulterers nor male prostitutes nor homosexual offenders nor thieves nor the greedy nor drunkards nor slanderers nor swindlers will inherit the kingdom of God. And that is what some of you were. But you were washed, you were sanctified, you were justified in the name of the Lord Jesus Christ and by the Spirit of our God.

He maintains that once you are in Christ you are a new creature: "Old things have passed away; behold all things are become new" (2 Corinthians 5:17).

Problems arise when we don't fast and pray to kill the sinful nature. If God says that it is forbidden, then it's forbidden. None of this rationalizing, "Well, I'll just do it and ask for forgiveness." You do it; you'll pay for it. And today, the consequences for being promiscuous could be deadly.

We are the generation to usher in the kingdom of God. We don't need to be stumbling in grace, questioning our salvation. We need to be about our Father's business, extending the royal scepter of God's grace to those who are perishing. The revival fire has been lit. We have great opposition at our door, but it is no match for the Holy Ghost. Once fire falls from Heaven and ignites the Church, not even the gates of hell can prevail against her (Matthew 16:18).

Back to the issue of accountability, a few years ago I was watching *Nightline*. Ted Koppel was doing a report on prisons, and after spending some time in solitary confinement, he asked the warden if he had any solutions to the increase in violent crime and prison overcrowding. The warden said, "Society has failed. The schools have failed. Parents have failed to teach that there are consequences for your actions." Saints, the Church has failed. Look at your own children and congregations. This cheap grace is the same grace that created the monster we called Nazi Germany. Fredrick Bonhoeffer will attest to this. This grace devoid of accountability, touted by psychology, is the doom of modern civilization. It may very well be the premise that enslaves the world and ushers in World War III, or in theological terms, "Armageddon."

Colin Powell put it best when he said, "America has lost her sense of shame." Nothing embarrasses us anymore; it is just the way things are. There is no fear of God. Hebrews tells us that "it is a fearful thing to fall into the hands of the living God" (Hebrews 10:31). Does God get angry? You bet He does. Sin and injustice cause the cup of His wrath to topple over (Revelation 14:10). As Revelation 16:9–11 reveals, it is the absence of repentance that intensifies the wrath of God.

Jesus tells us a parable of a man at a wedding feast who comes in without his wedding clothes and whom the Lord orders to be cast into outer darkness (Matthew 22:11–14). Revelation 19:8 reveals that the white linen wedding garments are the righteousness of the saints. Without tampering with the meaning, it means what it says: the righteous acts of the saints.

CHAPTER 4

THE END OF THE AGE

In Revelation 20:1–6, John reveals God's judgment at the end of the age:

> And I saw an angel coming down out of heaven, having the key to the Abyss and holding in his hand a great chain. He seized the dragon that ancient serpent who is the devil, or Satan, and bound him for a thousand years. He threw him into the Abyss, and locked and sealed it over him, to keep him from deceiving the nations anymore until the thousand years were ended. After that, he must be set free for a short time. I saw thrones on which were seated those who had been given authority to judge. And I saw the souls of those who had

been beheaded because of their testimony for Jesus and because of the word of God. They had not worshiped the beast or his image and had not received his mark on their foreheads or their hands. They came to life and reigned with Christ a thousand years. (The rest of the dead did not come to life until the thousand years were ended.) This is the first resurrection. Blessed and holy are those who have part in the first resurrection. The second death has no power over them, but they will be priests of God and of Christ and will reign with him for a thousand years.

The natural man is into survival. He wants to survive what is coming. In the 1999 school year, one of my students handed me a book. We were talking about the computer crisis, so her father sent me a copy: *Y2K Disaster 2,000: The Millennial Survival Guide*.

What was the "millennial bug"? It was claimed that on Friday night, December 31, 1999, at the stroke of midnight, what should become the year 2000 was to be coded 00 by the computers and would be understood by the computer to be 1900. Hence, everything computerized was to shut down. We learned that a lot of those bad things did not happen, and it may be attributed to the billions of dollars thrown at the problem.

However, countries that spent a lot less seemed to have had no problem either. (Just remember that in the world the natural man can not see the things of God, for they are spiritually discerned [see 1 Corinthians 2:14].)

People were panic-stricken. Many were starting to come back to God or at least inquiring. The world picked up on the Church's theme. The newspaper headlines in the store read: "Billy Graham thunders the end of the age. Doom and disaster are upon us." In 1999, the U.S. was engaged in a struggle in the very same region where WWI started and where WWII was waged in Bosnia and Sarejevo. The Chinese and the Russians were mad at us, the only two countries that have power to destroy us atomically. The world had a right to be scared.

Even the newspapers took full-page ads just in case the Christians were right. One article in the Sunday Living Section of the *Plain Dealer* newspaper was entitled, "Awaiting the Rapture." It was all about 1 Thessalonians 4:13–18 in which Christ removes His Church from the earth.

One thing I do know: it couldn't happen the way the world was expecting or anticipating that the age will end because: "They were all preparing." Jesus told us: "Behold I come like a thief in the night." The world will be clueless. The Word of God warns us through the epistles, "Behold I come as a thief in the night" (1 Thessalonians 5:1–6; Revelation 16:15; Revelation 3:3; and 2 Peter 3:10–14).

The Church that is ready is expecting to be raptured. Read Revelation 3:7–10. Jesus encouraged the church of Philadelphia in Revelation 3:10: "Because you have kept the word of my patience, I will keep you from the hour of temptation which is to try the whole world."

The church that is not ready can expect judgment. Jesus warned the church of Thyatira in Revelation 2:18–29:

> "To the angel in the church in Thyatira write: These are the words of the Son of God, whose eyes are like blazing fire and whose feet are like burnished bronze. I know your deeds, your love and faith, your service and perseverance and that you are now doing more than you did at first. Nevertheless, I have this against you: You tolerate that woman Jezebel, who calls herself a prophetess. By her teaching she misleads my servants into sexual immorality and the eating of food sacrificed to idols. I have given her time to repent of her immorality, but she is unwilling. So I will cast her on a bed of suffering, and I will make those who commit adultery with her

suffer intensely, unless they repent of their ways. I will strike her children dead. Then all the churches will know that I am he who searches hearts and minds, and I will repay each of you according to your deeds. Now I say to the rest of you in Thyatira, to you who do not hold to her teaching and have not learned Satan's so-called deep secrets (I will not impose any other burden on you): Only hold on to what you have until I come. To him who overcomes and does my will to the end, I will give authority over the nations—He will rule them with an iron scepter; He will dash them to pieces like pottery—just as I have received authority from my Father. I will also give him the morning star. He who has an ear, let him hear what the Spirit says to the churches."

My concern is not the world's prognosis but what does Jesus say will be the end? In Matthew 24:3–14, Jesus gives us an abbreviated end-time dissertation:

As Jesus was sitting on the Mount of Olives, the disciples came to him privately. "Tell us," they said, "when will this happen, and what will be the sign of your coming and of the end of the age?"

Jesus answered: "Watch out that no one deceives you. For many will come in my name, claiming, 'I am the Christ,' and will deceive many. You will hear of wars and rumors of wars, but see to it that you are not alarmed. Such things must happen, but the end is still to come. Nation will rise against nation, and kingdom against kingdom. There will be famines and earthquakes in various places. All these are the beginning of birth pains. Then you will be handed over to be persecuted and put to death, and you will be hated by all nations because of me. At that time many will turn away from the faith and will betray and hate each other, and many false prophets will appear and deceive many people. Because of the increase of wickedness, the love of most will grow cold, but he who stands firm to the end will be saved. And this gospel of the kingdom will be preached in the whole world as a testimony to all nations, and then the end will come."

Five Minutes 'til Midnight

Revelation 20:1–6:

And I saw an angel coming down out of heaven, having the key to the Abyss and holding in his hand a great chain. He seized the dragon, that ancient serpent, who is the devil, or Satan, and bound him for a thousand years. He threw him into the Abyss, and locked and sealed it over him, to keep him from deceiving the nations anymore until the thousand years ended. After that, he must be set free for a short time. I saw thrones on which were sealed those who had been given authority to judge. And I saw the souls of those who had been beheaded because of their testimony for Jesus and because of the Word of God. They had not worshiped the beast or his image and had not received his mark on their foreheads or their hands. They came to life and reigned with Christ a thousand years. (The rest of the dead did not come to life until the thousand years were ended.) This is the first resurrection. Blessed and holy are those who have part in the first resurrection. The second death has no power over them, but they will be priests of God and of Christ and will reign with Him for a thousand years.

- 6,000 years ago Adam was on the earth.
- 5,000 years ago Noah was on the earth.
- 4000 years ago Abraham was on the earth.
- 3,000 years ago David was on the earth.
- 2,000 years ago Christ invaded the earth. Hallelujah!
- 1,000 years ago the Church was the center of the earth.

Now on the edge of the millennium, the Church has lost its focus. Its power and influence has waned. She desires more the glitz and glamour of this world than streets of gold and gates of pearl. She is more interested in the stars of Hollywood than the Stars of heaven—Father, Son, and Holy Ghost. She has substituted talk show hosts and media influence for the Word of God and the presence of the Holy Ghost. The Church has lost her focus, and Christ must intervene. The politics of men are about to drag us into another world war. Pompous men and arrogance have replaced peace, hope, and love at the highest level.

The Most High shakes His head at the foolishness of man, and He is soon to say, "Enough."

Listen, it is not about clever words and education. Those are gifts like any other gift to be used by the Master's hand to build His kingdom. It is about His presence. The secret is His presence, and you can only get that by sitting quietly before Him. Some of the most powerful men to walk the earth were the apostles. These were uneducated, unlearned men who on the Day of Pentecost spoke over twenty languages by divine power (Acts 2:1–21). When they came into the room, Jesus came with them. Long after He had been crucified and resurrected, they knew how to enter His presence. It is not some Pentecostal formula but simply allowing the holiness of God to pervade your being and the truth of God to consume your mind. (The problem with man is he always seeks to justify himself, rather than admit he's wrong and move on.) Remember, the law came through Moses, but grace and truth came through Jesus Christ. We must not allow the compromise of our generation and the compromise of our hearts to sidestep God's truth. Remember, He is coming for all those who are waiting and watching for His appearing and who know and love the truth. Amen.

The American Dilemma

The world is the way it is because of Christ in it. It would be better if we had blocked the antichrist forces that sought to erode the fabric that brought America prosperity in the 1950s. It is the call of the Great Commission that has compelled believers in Christ to share their faith. As hypocritical as some of the Western nations of the world have been, it was their conscience and the conscience of their citizens that brought us universal suffrage, civil rights, women's rights, and human rights. It was the economic embargoes and economic boycotts that changed nations like South Africa and caused even the

Soviet Union to admire prosperity and success. It is the blessing of God and not the ingenuity of man that has brought us to this point. America has forgotten that it is the favor of God because of the furtherance of the gospel. And as our leaders and our people lose this focus, so will go our prosperity. We have almost reached the point of no return. We have one option: Sincere revival or imminent judgment. The clouds of judgment are beginning to roll.

Judgment is Coming!

The Lord woke me up one day and told me: "Judgment is coming!"

My sister called me right after the Lord woke me up, and I could only repeat to her the same thing. She said that she was flying back from Amsterdam to New York, and the Lord spoke the same thing to her. As she looked at the clouds, she said they looked like "clouds of judgment."

Billy Graham, David Wilkerson, and business and technology are all saying the same thing. (I received three messages as confirmation.) In Billy Graham's May 1999 issue of *Decision Magazine*, the title reads: "The End of the World is Coming: Are you Ready?" David Wilkerson's May 10, 1999, *Times Square Church's Pulpit Series* message was Revelation 12:12: "Therefore

rejoice you heavens and you who dwell in them!
But woe to the earth and the sea, because the
devil has gone down to you! He is filled with fury,
because he knows that his time is short."

For some only the almighty dollar will get
their attention. Well, *US News and World Report*
in the October 12, 1998, section of Business and
Technology, featured an article entitled, "Who
Lost Capitalism? As economies reel, support for
free capital flow erodes." It talks about all the
economies of the world failing and our inability
to stop it.

I want to go back to Billy Graham's introduc-
tion because I believe that it is perfectly timed for
this generation. In his May 1999 *Decision* article,
Billy Graham states: "The End of the World is
Coming: Are You Ready?" The world-renowned
evangelist declares:

> People ask me, "Do you really believe that
> Jesus Christ is going to come back to this
> earth again?" Yes, I do. The Bible teaches
> that Jesus is coming again. And I don't see
> any other hope for the world because we're
> heading toward a catastrophe in our world.
> The Bible says, "There shall come in the last
> days scoffers, walking after their own lusts,
> And saying, Where is the promise of his
> coming? For since the fathers fell asleep, all

things continue as they were from the beginning of the creation. For this they willingly are ignorant of, that by the word of God the heavens were of old, and the earth standing out of water and in the water: Whereby the world that then was, being overflowed with water, perished: But the heavens and the earth, which are now, by the same word are kept in store, reserved unto fire against the day of judgment and perdition of ungodly men."

—2 Peter 3:3–7

In other words, there's going to come a judgment on this earth, and it will be a judgment of fire.

For years people believed that the threat of a nuclear holocaust was diminishing, but nuclear tests have again raised fears that an incident somewhere in the world can still plunge us into a global catastrophe.

Scientists say that we're closer now to a world destruction than at any other time in the past. Almost all of us would agree that the end of the world as we know it is a possibility scientifically.

The Word of God speaks of the certainties of the end of the world. Jesus said, "As the days of [Noah] were, so shall also the coming of the Son of man be" (Matthew 24:37). What were the days of Noah like? And is there a parallel now?

One word that is used to describe the days of Noah is wickedness. The people were very wicked: Every imagination of their thoughts was evil (Genesis 6:5). It seems as if they stayed awake at night thinking up new ways to do evil. It was a world in which marriage was abused. The people were corrupt and were violent (Genesis 6:11–12). It was a world in which violence prevailed: murders, wars, insurrections.

It was a world in which there was a lot of religion, but it was a decadent religion. They were preoccupied with things, and they were taken up with their everyday living. They didn't have time for God.

It was a world that was threatened by the judgment of God. God had warned them, "Unless you repent and turn from your sins and change your ways, you're going to face the judgment."

—Genesis 6:6–7, 13

But in the middle of all that, there stood one man. God had said, "With all this sin and violence and corruption, I'm going to destroy the whole world" (Genesis 6:13). But He didn't do it because of that one man who was going against the tide of that day. His name was Noah. In all that corruption Noah dared to walk with God. Noah believed in God, and true faith determined how Noah lived.

And true faith determines how you live. Do you worship God in your home? Do you have Bible reading and prayer?

The Bible says, "By faith Noah, being warned of God of things not seen as yet, moved with fear, prepared [a ship]" (Hebrews 11:7). God told Noah to build a ship out in the desert (Genesis 6:14–16). Noah had no place to sail the ship, but he was to build it.

And God said, "I'm going to save you and your family when the destruction comes."

—Genesis 6:17–20

So Noah started out, and judgment eventually came. God spoke to Noah again and said, "Noah, I'm going to give the world seven more days, and then the flood will come."

—Genesis 7:4

Today the only bright spot on the horizon of this world is the promise of the Coming again of Christ, the Messiah. We can't go on much longer morally. We can't go on much longer scientifically. The technology that was supposed to save us is ready to destroy us. New weapons are being made all the time, including chemical and biological weapons.

In Isaiah 66 we read that "the Lord will come with fire, and with his chariots like a whirlwind, to render his anger with fury" (Isaiah 66:15). In the New Testament we read that Christ said, "I go to prepare a place for you. And if I go and prepare a place for you, I will come again, and receive you unto my self; that where I am, there [you] may be also."

—John 14:2–3

Jesus promised that He is coming back, and we are to "comfort one another with these words" (1 Thessalonians 4:18). We're not to wait in terror because as believers we have the hope of the Coming again of Christ.

When Jesus was getting ready to go back to the Father, some of the disciples and His friends from Galilee were watching and waiting. Two angels said, "Why stand ye gazing up into heaven? This same Jesus, which is taken up from you into heaven, shall so come in like manner as ye have seen him go into heaven" (Acts 1:11). That is God's promise to us, to you and me.

It has been 2,000 years since then. Why hasn't He come? The disciples asked the same thing, and Jesus said, "It is not for you to know the times or the seasons, which the Father hath put in his own power" (Acts 1:7). (Note: The disciples asked, "Lord, are you at this time going to restore the kingdom to Israel?" To this He replied, it is not for them to know. The end times has a season and the Bible says that we in this generation will know it, however we will not know the day, (i.e., Matthew 24:32–44).

Jesus said, "Of that day and hour knoweth no man, no, not the angels of heaven, but my Father only" (Matthew 24:36). Don't guess and speculate. We don't know. It may be a thousand years from now, or it may be tomorrow.

When is the end of the world coming? The end of the world is coming for you the moment you die, and that could be at any time for any of us. We never know.

How will Christ come? "The Lord himself shall descend from heaven with a shout, with the voice of the archangel, and with the trump of God: and the dead in Christ shall rise first."

—1 Thessalonians 4:16

Are you ready for that if that happened today? God said, "Prepare to meet thy God" (Amos 4:12). The Bible says, "Then we which are alive and remain shall be caught up together with them in the clouds, to meet the Lord in the air: and so shall we ever be with the Lord" (1 Thessalonians 4:17). We're going to go as believers and meet Him. Jesus said, "Be ready: for in such an hour as ye think not the Son of man cometh, He will come."

—Matthew 24:44

Again: "Judgment is coming?"

Somebody sent me a transcript of this message by radio announcer, Paul Harvey, about the problems in American schools that led to the incident at Columbine:

I'll tell you that America's overall problem is that she doesn't fear God. The kids have embodied this philosophy, and God had sent us warning after warning that if we don't stand up and say thus says the Lord: "It's going to get worse!"

The Bible teaches that there are principles of blessing and curses for a nation:

In Deuteronomy 28's principles of blessings and curses, the Word of God states that if you hearken or listen to the voice of the Lord and obey all His commands, that every blessing imaginable will be yours. In the same light, it says if you choose not to listen to His commands and disregard His guidance and correction, then all the curses imaginable will follow you.

The Bible calls the fear of the Lord the beginning of wisdom (Proverbs 1:7).

Dr. Stowell of Moody put an emphasis on the beginning of wisdom and noted that it is the one thing that is forbidden in school. So all education is gone to pot because we can't discuss the foundation principle out of which all morality flows.

My sister and I were talking about things to come. She said she packed up the baby in the car and went to visit a girlfriend in upstate New Jersey. She said that her friend's husband is a computer software consultant technician, and she joked how her friends were all worried about Y2K. They said to stock up on food and water once the date changes, and she laughed. She noticed that he didn't laugh.

She said that he said, "I'm not going to do that, but you see that tree over there? I'm going to put a backup generator right there."

She said, "What are your concerns?" He said, "It is those damn electric companies. They are not compliant. Everything electric is going to shut down. Only companies that are rich enough can afford generators that big, and all the little supply companies are going to mess up this country."

Well, we know that we were able to head off Y2K, but nothing could prepare us for 9/11. Terrorism is just that: "unimaginable, intimidating fear via force and violence."

America's judgment is coming out of her own mouth: The devil and Hollywood have picked up on it, and we're in for a ride.

Let me show you some of the things that the Bible says are going to happen and of which Hollywood has picked up on and of which the devil is fully aware:

1. *The Titanic (America thought that she was unsinkable). Most of you know that this movie is about the unsinkable ship that sank. The Lord says in 1 Thessalonians 5:3: "When they say peace and safety, then sudden destruction cometh as upon a woman in travail; and they shall not escape."*

2. *Deep Impact (America's fascination with natural disaster). This movie is about a meteorite hitting the earth and causing cataclysmic disaster. In Revelation 6:12–14 and Revelation 16:17–21, the Bible tells us about an earthquake to come like never before in the history of man:*

I watched as he opened the sixth seal. There was a great earthquake. The sun turned black like sackcloth made of goat hair, the whole moon turned blood red, and the stars in the sky fell to earth, as late figs drop from a fig tree when shaken by a strong wind. The sky receded like a scroll, rolling up, and every mountain and island was removed from its place.

The seventh angel poured out his bowl into the air, and out of the temple came a loud voice from the throne, saying, "It is finished." Then there came flashes of lightning, rumblings, peals of thunder and a severe earthquake. No earthquake like it has ever occurred since man has been on the earth, so tremendous was the quake. The great city split into three parts, and the cities of the nations collapsed. God remembered Babylon the Great and gave her the cup filled with the wine of the fury of His wrath. Every island fled away and the mountains could not be found. From the sky huge hailstones of about a hundred pounds each fell upon men. And they cursed God on account of the plague of hail, because the plague was so terrible.

3. ***Devil's Advocate** (This is Hollywood's fascination with evil and the Antichrist).*

This movie freaked my brother out so badly that he wanted me to watch it to tell him if it was really going to happen. (The movie twisted the Book of Revelation, but let's see what God says in Revelation 13:4–8.)

Men worshipped the dragon because he had given authority to the beast, and they also worshipped the beast and asked, "Who is like the beast? Who can make war against him?" (The beast obviously has superior war powers). The beast was given a mouth to utter proud words and blasphemies and to exercise his authority for forty-two months. He opened his mouth to blaspheme God, and to slander his name and his dwelling place and those who live in heaven. He was given power to make war against the saints and to conquer them. And he was given authority over every tribe, people, language and nation. All inhabitants of the earth will worship the beast—all whose names have not been written in the book of life belonging to the Lamb that was slain from the creation of the world. (For further reading, see Revelation 13 and 17.)

4. *Independence Day (All of our major cities and monuments are destroyed in*

this movie.) (I will not watch it because things I watch tend to come true.) Revelation 9:13–21:

The sixth angel sounded his trumpet, and I heard a voice coming from the horns of the golden altar that is before God. It said to the sixth angel who had the trumpet, "Release the four angels who are bound at the great river Euphrates." And the four angels who had been kept ready for this very hour and day and month and year were released to kill a third of mankind. The number of the mounted troops was two hundred million. I heard their number. The horses and riders I saw in my vision looked like this: Their breastplates were fiery red, dark blue, and yellow as sulfur. The heads of the horses resembled the heads of lions, and out of their mouths came fire, smoke and sulfur that came out of their mouths. The power of the horses was in their mouths and in their tails; for their tails were like snakes, having heads with which they inflict injury. The rest of mankind that were not killed by these plagues still did not repent of the work of their hands; they did not stop worshipping demons, and idols of gold, silver, bronze, stone and wood—idols that cannot see or hear or walk. Nor did they repent of their murders, their magic arts, their sexual immorality or their thefts.

Right now missiles are aimed at all our major cities, and we are angering the two nations that have the power to destroy us, and America doesn't directly appear in prophecy. She has begun to deny His name in her schools and in her courts, and He promises to deny the name of anyone who denies Him.

As America reels from 9/11, one of the greatest revivals known to men is going to sweep the country. The churches will not be able to contain the converts. After the novelty wears off (about a year and a half), and the smoke clears and the dust settles, the true converts, God's holy remnant, will remain in the Church, and the rest will go back to their wicked ways or indifference of business as usual.

On the night that Bill Clinton gave the order to begin the bombing of the Serb stronghold in Kosovo (March 1999), two stars collided in the heavens. This would have been an ominous sign to the ancient scholars of the stars.

Those managing foreign policy have set us on a dangerous course of backing causes and ignoring the fragile peace of the global community. Having the Chinese and the Russians angry at us in the same week is not wise. In the process, we accidentally bombed the Chinese embassy and failed to get Russia's support for our campaign. According to the Russians, the peace process has been set back by decades.

What about all the missiles aimed at US cities, the Russian sale of missiles to our enemies, and the toppling of the government of Iraq? The Russians sell missiles because that's all they have left to sell; their economy is in shambles. Our toppling of the government of Iraq without building an international coalition has set foreign relations back thirty years. What precedent have we set for the future of foreign relations? Are we to police the world? What is to stop other superpowers from acting accordingly?

Prayer and War

- *We had prayer in school during every war we fought but the **Vietnam War.***
- *In **World War I**, 1917–1921, all of the women and children were praying for their husbands and daddies and brothers to come home.*
- *In **World War II**, 1939–1945, every mother and child in America went to church*

and prayed. They prayed in school. (Remember the movie, It's a Wonderful Life? George Bailey prayed, and he cried like everyone else. He also went to church like everyone else.)

- **The Korean War** *(1950–1958; there were few casualties). This was the family generation. Everyone respected God as the final authority and upheld the Bible as His standard. School was a safe place, and today's talk show discussions were taboo. By the time of the Vietnam War, they had taken prayer out of schools. The country's leading institutions began teaching atheism, and we lost the war and 56,000 young men. And today we're still trying to figure out how.*

- *The* **Gulf War of 1991.** *I don't know how many of you remember or would have paid attention, but at that time, Saddam Hussein had the second largest army in the world. The night before the war, the newscasters, who are known atheists, were scared, as was George Bush, Sr. The newscasters were telling people to pray, and George Bush (Daddy Bush) called Billy Graham to spend the night* *at the White House. A very wise move on his part. Today, we are in trouble. Most people don't know how to pray or who to pray to.*

Falling Stars, Meteorite Showers, and Heavenly Blasts

For thousands of years, man has looked to the stars (astronomy) in order to prophesy the future. Daniel and his Hebrew brothers studied the stars (Daniel 1:19–21). The wise men saw the birth of Christ (Matthew 2:1–7), and Jesus foretold ominous signs in the heavenlies before His return (Matthew 24:29–31). Falling stars, meteorite showers, and heavenly blasts were all onerous, malevolent signs of things to come. On March 31, 1999, we had a "blue" moon (two full moons). This is only the second time in that century that we have had two months with two full moons each. The last time that happened was in 1915; hence, the phrase, "Once in a blue moon."

But what was going on in 1915? All historians and students of history know that the world was engaged in a world war brought on by a Serbian grandstander who shot the Archduke Ferdinand, who was heir to the Austrian-Hungarian throne.

Presently, under the second bimonthly blue moon in history for the second time in history, the world has been engaged in conflict brought on by a Serbian grandstander whose only concern is his own self-interests. The first Serbian action precipitated World War I. This present world initiative has greatly divided the fragile world coalition in NATO. A most important ally, Russia, necessary for world peace, is growing cold toward us.

Where Is Russia in Prophecy?

Biblical prophecy tells us that Russia's Old Testament provinces of Meshech and Tubal will "think evil thoughts" and set their faces against Jerusalem and the nation of Israel.

Ezekiel chapters thirty-eight and thirty-nine: According to these Scriptures, Russia will attack Israel in order to seize her livestock, provision, and wealth. Miraculously, a force of fire, hailstones, and brimstone will wipe out the invading army, leaving a stench of corpses and carcasses, which will compel the Israelites to spend the next seven years burying the dead. We the United States are not specifically mentioned in prophecy. Either we (the US) are Israel (see Davidic Covenant, chapter seven), or we are part of the beast's kingdom and system. Who-ever has Star Wars, a strategic defense shield over the nation, will rule the world (Revelation 13). The patriot missile is the closest thing that I have ever seen to Star Wars, yet it is the beast and the Antichrist's kingdom that possess it (Revelation 13). (The patriot missile was first used strategically in the Gulf War to shoot down Iraqi scud missiles before they hit their target via a heat-seeking mechanism.)

Two Stars Collide

Remarkably, the stars are coinciding with earthly events. At the same time that President Clinton, acting through NATO, was lighting up the skies in Kosovo, the heavens were putting on their own display. The scientists reported that on March 24 and 25, 1999, two stars collided, creating a spectacle never before seen. Listen, this is an omen. The Hebrews, the Greeks, and the Romans would have taken this as a bad sign. Could the two stars colliding be the collision of the nuclear superpowers, the United States and the Soviet Union? Our foreign policy and the Middle East situation seem to be driving us further apart.

St. Malachi's Papal Predictions for the Catholic Church

St. Malachi, a twelfth-century prophetic Irish priest, predicted the characteristics of all popes until the return of Christ. According to Malachi, there are only two popes left to follow John Paul II. The last pope will be named Peter. The recent pope, John Paul II, whom Malachi described as "the labor of the sun," was the first pope in over 450 years who was not Italian and who previously had worked with his hands. John Paul II—God bless him—feared the arrival of the Antichrist's pope, or Peter II. Valiantly, John Paul II clung to life, fearing the succession of a cardinal who no longer professes that Jesus Christ is the Son of God. His prophecies were in line with those of St. Malachi, a devout Irish priest from the twelfth century, who predicted the last three hundred popes. According to St. Malachi, Pope John Paul I was the pope "between crescent moons" who mysteriously died after a month. The first quarter and last quarter of moon (the crescents) occur within each month. Pope John Paul I's reign was only to be one month.

Pope John Paul II was actually in a work camp during the Nazi occupation of Poland. Unmistakably, he is "the labor of the sun" and has proven to be the "labor of the Son" as a goodwill ambassador for Christ around the world. According to St. Malachi, the next pope will either be the pope of the olive branch, signifying that he will attempt to be a peacemaker or the pope with the olive skin, signifying a Latino, African, or dark complexion. After this pope will come Peter, or Peter II in name succession, signifying the end of the age, the ushering in of the antichrist period and the establishment of God's kingdom in accordance with Revelation, chapter seventeen through chapter twenty-one.

It's about closing time, boys; never before has man had the power to destroy himself and everything else with it.

Today, Iran, Iraq, and all of these other crazy little dictatorships are racing to get the bomb. Right now, all you have to do is take instructions off the Internet. In the name of God, they would blow themselves up, and the rest of us, kamikaze-style. First Peter 3:10–14 says the earth will burn with fervent heat. I want to know that I am on the right side of God.

If salvation was something money could buy, the rich would live and the poor would die.

What's wrong? There is such a selfishness today in society and politics. The poor have been all but abandoned to the mercy of this cruel world. Oh, but God's eyes are on the poor and His ears are ever attentive to their cry.

Too Busy to Die

In Luke 14:16–21 (and Matthew 22:1–14 coinciding), the Lord tells a parable about the kingdom of Heaven. In this parable, the Lord has called a great supper, or wedding feast, for the marriage of His Son; however, the people invited were too busy to come. They were busy buying and selling real estate, trading merchandise (business), or busy with married life (sound familiar?). The Lord was angry and disinvited all those with excuses. He then sent His servants into the streets, into the highways and hedges to get the poor, the maimed, the crippled, and the blind to fill His table. (This should sound familiar, for how many excuses do you hear from so-called believers when invited to something for the Lord?) Is this what Jesus called the end of the age?

There are no surprises that God has not already addressed. Men never stockpile weapons without intending to use them. Never before has man had the power to destroy the earth and himself. Never before have we had so many unstable and hostile nations clamoring for nuclear power. Is this what Jesus called the end of the age?

Why should Christ return now in this present age?

Why should Christ return now as opposed to any other time in history? I must reiterate because never before in the history of time has man had the power to destroy himself and everyone and everything else. And never has the danger of that power falling into the wrong hands been greater. If you haven't guessed yet, I'm talking about the power of nuclear weapons—weapons of mass destruction. Iran and Iraq and many of the other Arab and Third World countries are racing toward Armageddon. India and Pakistan have already arrived, as they so cordially demonstrated to the world. It is a dangerous time to be living in, yet exciting, as we watch prophecy unfold.

"When ye see all these things, know that it is near, even at your very doors." According to Jesus, "And this generation shall not pass until all these things be fulfilled" (see Matthew 24:33-34). All one needs is to know current history to see prophecy unfold:

1. *On May 14, 1948, Israel prophetically became a nation again and a physical reference point of biblical prophecy. (Israel as a nation did not exist for over 1800 years).*

2. *In 1967, the Israeli army captured Jerusalem, ending the biblical reference period in Luke called "the times of the Gentiles," catapulting Israel into the national spotlight (Luke 21:24).*

3. *China and Russia, the two nations that differ the most with the US ideologically, are prophesied to flabbergast the world by their actions: Russia attacking Israel (Ezekiel 38 and 39); China attacking the Antichrist's kingdom (Revelation 9:14–18).*

4. *The Bible prophesies a great addiction, or obsession, with drugs in the end times. The word for "sorcery" in Revelation is "pharmakia," which is our word for "drug." The Bible says that they would not repent of their sorcery or drugs (Revelation 19 and 21). God says that if you are under this influence, you will not enter the kingdom of Heaven.*

5. *We are at the end of Daniel's prophecy: the revitalization of the Old Roman*

Empire in the United States of Europe, or the European Economic Community. The Antichrist's kingdom is supposed to come out of the Old Roman Empire (Daniel 2 and 7; Revelation 13 and 17). This is summed up as a one-world government and a one-world currency in a New World order.

Where Is China's Place in Prophecy?

According to Revelation 16:12-16 and Revelation 9:13-21, the great Euphrates River will supernaturally dry up during the reign of the anti christ and the Wrath of God. The kings of the East will march a vast army of two hundred million (200,000,000) armed with the latest military artillery and technology. (Only China has an army this large. Napoleon said that "China was a sleeping giant; when she wakes up look out"). This army will wipe out one-third of the men in their march across the Euphrates.

The kings of the earth will be demonically deceived by the anti christ and his false miracles and will be led to Armageddon to do battle against the Lord Almighty. (Note: China is still Communist and atheist. Deception is easy.) China will survive a worldwide depression by using their army to take what they want.

CHAPTER 5

OUR PRESENT STATE

The Time We Live In

The Bible speaks concerning the time we live in. In Nahum 2:4, chariots (cars) jostle one against another. They appear to be "flaming torches moving like lightning." This is the car at night. Read it for yourself. It was written around 663 B.C.

"Multitudes, multitudes in the valley of decision" (Joel 2:14). There has never been a greater sense of lostness, emptiness, and loneliness in the world. This is the age we live in. The Word says: "My people are destroyed for lack of knowledge....seeing thou has forgotten the law of God, I will also forget thy children" (Hosea 4:6–7). Could this be why we have a generation completely devoid of morals?

There is a connection, folks, between following God's laws and raising good children. The children may go off on their own for a while, but they always come back to what they were taught: "Train up a child in the way that he should go so that when he is old he will not depart from it" (Proverbs 22:6).

Now, let's recap some of the facts that put us squarely in the realm of end-time prophecy.

According to prophecy and Britain's own coronation statements, Elizabeth II may be the last monarch to complete her reign. (See "Davidic Covenant, chapter seven.")

According to the prophecy of St. Malachi, the Irish, twelfth-century cleric, there are only two popes to follow Pope John Paul II, who was the Labor of the Sun or Son: first the pope with the olive branch or the olive skin, and the last pope whose name will be "Peter." (See St. Malachi's Papal Predictions.)

"When you see Jerusalem surrounded by armies, know that its desolation and devastation is near" (Luke 21:20). Jerusalem was surrounded by armies in the WWI campaign and the WWII campaign. The Gulf War again saw Jerusalem surrounded by the armies of the world. Presently, in this endless war on terror, Jerusalem is surrounded by armies; however, the nations surrounding Israel are racing, jostling, and vying for atomic power.

"And this gospel must be preached as a witness to all nations and then the end shall come" (Matthew 24:14). Jesus foretold the international preaching of the gospel before His return (Matthew 24:14), like what the Reverend Billy Graham has done his entire life.

"This generation shall not pass until all these things be fulfilled" (Matthew 24:34). (Note: Israel is the centerpiece for all biblical prophecy. It is God's reference point—the birthplace of Abraham, Isaac, and Jacob, and of the Lord Jesus Christ. In 1948 Israel became a nation. In 1967 Jerusalem was turned over to the Jews. 1) We are the generation that has seen these things. This generation will not pass until all is fulfilled. 2) The times of the Gentiles are fulfilled once Jerusalem is back in Jewish hands. This happened in 1967 [see Luke 21:24].)

Judgment on the kingdom of Judah will be the same judgment on America:

1. *Like Judah, America has despised the law of the Lord.*

2. *Like Judah, America has not kept His commandments.*

3. *Like Judah, America has been snared by lies (Jeremiah 44:1–14, 23:10–20).*

God promised to rain down fire. It could be literal or a terrorist attack. *Fire is fire. Sodom and Gomorrah were destroyed by literal fire.* Our only hope is to defer God's judgment by turning back to Him before He unleashes His wrath. Wrath is coming, but God knows how to spare His children from wrath (1 Thessalonians 4:16–18; 2 Peter 3:10). The earth shall burn with fervent heat.

The British Monarchy

Elizabeth may be the last monarch to complete her reign. (*God save the queen! Long live the queen!*) Why? Because the coronation stone—the stone upon which kings were crowned for a thousand years—was sent back to Scotland. Notice, we have entered a new millennium, and this was done a few years ago.

Don't Blame Bill Clinton

Don't blame Bill Clinton.

The Church has failed to stand up and be the Church and call sin, sin. She has failed to stand up and be the bride that Christ told us she must be at His return. She has parsed words, split infinitives, and redefined terms such as "holiness," "righteousness," and "truth." "Holiness" does not mean holiness, and "righteousness" does not mean righteousness. It has been redefined to mean "only that which comes from Christ" rather than the walk and actions of the believer's life in Christ. Remember, we are saved by grace, through faith, for good works (Ephesians 2:8–9).

The Church, for the last twenty to thirty years, has been gradually stripping the believer of all accountability for his actions. This philosophy that it doesn't matter what you do or how you live as long as you profess Christ is damning millions to hell, creating a seared conscience (1 Timothy 4:1–2).

Bill Clinton is a product of the apostate Church. All of you who wanted him removed from office and who were sorely disappointed when your human efforts failed must be reminded of the sovereignty of God. "God sets up kings and removes kings at his discretion" (Psalm 75:6–7). God has used Bill Clinton to expose the racism and hypocrisy in this country whether directly or indirectly. His transparency and nature have been God's method of getting our attention. God is speaking to us from the

"Bully Pulpit"—His Way. "Thy kingdom come, Thy will be done" is finally coming to fruition and replacing man's twisted reinterpreted prayer of "my will be done till thy kingdom come." This is what the Church is saying every time it denies His holiness and our need to walk holy however miserably we fail. God has said, "I am the Lord, I change not" (Malachi 3:6). We have to change, because He (God) is not going to. He expects us to change and not provoke Him.

The Church cannot be upset with Bill Clinton, because the Church has been speaking Bill Clinton's language for a long time. A.W. Tozer warned that the Church was headed toward a liberal theology where one could live however one wants to live and still be saved. Nowhere in the Bible is this found.

In 1 Corinthians, chapter six, the apostle Paul warned vehemently against such heresy. The Corinthian church thought they could "believe" with their mouth by profession of faith and fornicate, or live hedonistically with their bodies. Paul lifted up the righteous requirement of God for the believer as the standard for all in Christ and God.

Do you not know that the wicked will not inherit the kingdom of God? Do not be deceived: Neither the sexually immoral nor idolaters nor adulterers nor male prostitutes nor homosexual offenders nor thieves nor the greedy nor drunkards nor slanderers nor swindlers will inherit the kingdom of God. And that is what some of you were. But you were washed, you were sanctified, you were justified in the name of the Lord Jesus Christ and by the Spirit of our God.

—1 Cor. 6:9-11

Note: He says, "and such 'were' some of you" (past tense), but Christ has washed you and sanctified you and justified you by His Spirit. Now we have a new nature, we are new creatures. It is not to say that we cannot make a mistake, but the mistakes are minor compared to the good coming out of us from knowing Christ.

See, the Church led President Clinton the wrong way. The same interpretation that President Clinton used to defend himself in that "political fiasco" of the century is the same way the evangelical church interprets the Bible. Everywhere it says "righteousness" or "holiness," the Church interprets that as meaning the importation of Christ's righteousness to them. Regardless of the text or the exegesis (the biblical interpretation of the text from the original language), the Church fights to maintain that it is sinful and can have no righteousness apart from the righteousness of Christ. This is heresy, and from it has spun all types of false theology such as, "Well, if Jeffrey Dahmer can make it, I know I can make it," or, "If Hitler repented at the last minute, he can be saved." It is heresy to say that holiness and righteousness are not attributes that God requires of His children. It is heresy to say that a believer is not required to be righteous. Remember in the book of Revelations, along with the book of life is a book of deeds. If it did not matter how you lived—but only what you believed—there would be no need for a book of deeds or works (See Revelation 20:12-15). Jesus said, "You will know them (believers) by their fruit. A good tree bears good fruit, and a corrupt tree bears evil fruit. A good tree cannot bring forth evil fruit; neither can a corrupt tree bring forth good fruit." This is Jesus, people, out of His own words. He says, "You will know them by their fruits, their actions, their deeds." This same Jesus also said, "If you love me, keep my commandments" (John 14:15). This same statement reads: If you don't love me, then don't keep my commandments. Herein lies accountability and responsibility, which the Church wants to deny itself. What are His commandments? "Love the Lord your God with all you heart, mind, soul, and strength and love your neighbor as yourself" (Luke 10:27–28).

Two Justice Systems

What has long been known in the black community was brought out in the O.J. Simpson trial. In America, there have been two justice systems: one for whites and one for African Americans and Hispanics. If this were not the truth, Johnnie Cochran would not have been able to play the race card. Johnnie Cochran's claim to fame is that he knows how to shock the courtroom with the truth—a skill that Chief Justice Earl Warren admired in Justice Thurgood Marshall. In the city of Cleveland, we had sixty police officers that were indicted for drug trafficking with the Mafia. The next major news story in Cleveland was that police officers weren't paid enough, and that is what caused the whole mess. One would wonder if the police officers received the same sentence as twenty-year-old African American and Hispanic males. To quote the famed Civil Rights leader, "Injustice anywhere is a threat to Justice everywhere" (Martin Luther King).

Truth Screams from Heaven

Whenever you see no resolution to tragedies or murders or deep questions that continue for decades, be it the assassinations of Lincoln and JFK, the outpouring of emotion for Princess

Diana, or the death of Marilyn Monroe, there is some truth that is crying out from the grave—like the blood of righteous Abel in Genesis—for justice. Many have heard of the similarities between Lincoln and JFK's assassinations: Lincoln's secretary was named Kennedy and Kennedy's secretary was named Lincoln, and the similarities go on and on. Lincoln's assassin ran from a theatre to a warehouse; whereas, Kennedy's assassin ran from a warehouse to a theatre. Well, there is one similarity that stands out as possibly the key to answering the question of conspiracy: both vice presidents were named Johnson. It is worth a full-scale media investigation.

If we could take a sledgehammer to jealousy, fear, competition, and strife, we could end all wars and bigotry, racism, murder, and strife. Christ does that through the Beatitudes as He re-teaches man how to live: To love our enemies and to do good to those that spitefully use and persecute us; to bless those who curse us and let God bring them to judgment (swiftly, He will do it in these last days). This is why the Arabs and the Jews cannot get along. Strict Orthodox Judaism and Islam teach revenge. Christianity teaches forgiveness. An Arab acquaintance once said to me in the midst of a discussion, "I know, I know, you Christians believe in forgiveness."

I said, "Well, it would solve your problem with Jewish people." He is from Iraq. Now, as the debates rage over capital punishment, I believe justice demands "a life for a life." It would be an affront to all justice to allow murderers to go free. However, the disproportionate number of African Americans on death row says something about our justice system and the cruel environment of a lot of the African-American communities.

The Church in a Ditch

Jesus said, "If the blind follow the blind, they both fall in a ditch." The Book of Galatians is God's treaty via the apostle Paul against tradition and ritual. Some men called Judaizers were perverting the gospel that Paul had preached, teaching the Galatian Christians that they had to observe circumcision, calendar dates, and other Jewish rules. Paul maintains that this was not the gospel that he preached; the gospel (his gospel) is a gospel of faith. This is the line that Paul has drawn; this is where he stops.

However, today, many ministries of the gospel are using Galatians to preach a gospel of grace void of accountability and responsibility—a dangerous once-saved, always-saved proposition. In this very book, Paul himself warned: that they that continue in the works of the flesh "shall not inherit the kingdom of God," for those that have come to Christ have "crucified the flesh with its affections and lusts" (Galatians 5:21, 24).

Please read the text for yourself and see if that is what is being preached in your church: "Walk in the Spirit and you shall not fulfill the lust of the flesh" (see Galatians 5:16–24).

The problem with the doctrine is that it lets Christ down. The Church is constantly affirming that this gospel that they preach has no power to sanctify. They say it has a power to save but no power to sanctify, or make holy, or separate, for God's use. The Church is constantly affirming its sinful state rather than its sanctified, justified state (Romans 8; Ephesians 2; Galatians 5). This has led to great confusion within the Church with regard to repentance and salvation. Salvation has boiled down to a profession—a people who get caught rather than a life-changing, 180-degree turn around. Then we hear statements like, "If Jeffrey Dahmer, mass murderer and cannibal, can make it, I know I can make it." We don't know if Jeffrey Dahmer made it. The word is that he was continuing his homosexual affairs in prison before he was murdered.

Let's look at what Jesus said. Jesus said, "You will know them by their fruits. A good tree bears good fruit, and an evil tree bears evil fruit. An evil tree cannot bring forth good fruit; neither can a good tree bring forth evil fruit" (Matthew 7:15–20).

Now, King David throughout his entire life brought forth good fruit. One major slip and he committed adultery and murder, which he paid for dearly the rest of his life. His son raped his daughter; one son murdered another; his nephew murdered the murderers. One third of his kingdom died in an earthquake (2 Samuel chapters eleven through twenty-four). Even after this David was truly repentant. His heart was right toward God. Today we are calling every profession salvation. Jesus says, "Show me the fruits."

If we preach a weak grace—that is, grace without accountability—then we will have a weak walk, which leads to a weak testimony and the common criticism: "Those church people are some of the biggest hypocrites. They sin all week, only to go to church on Sunday to look pious."

We must remember the words of Jesus, "Ye have not chosen me, but I have chosen you, and ordained you, that ye should go and bring forth fruit, and that your fruit should remain: that whatsoever ye shall ask of the Father in my name, he may give it to you. These things I command you that ye love one another" (John 15:16–17).

Concentrate on verse sixteen and answer this question: How are we to bring forth fruit if our testimony is "toilet paper"—good for nothing but to be flushed after one use. Saints, fellow Christians, you know very well that people will disregard what you say if they find you to be untruthful. My father's mother, bless her heart, would always say: "What you do speaks so loud, I can't hear what you say!" She has long since passed away, yet her words continue to echo in my heart and mind.

Even if I mess up and fail like King David, that doesn't change God. His righteous demands are still the same, and He demands a righteous walk and accountability from His children even if they fail miserably and in the process have to repent to be back in right standing with Him. His truth remains the same, as King David well knew. He, the Lord, was holy before David fell into sin and remains holy until the present day. The Scriptures tell us to, "be holy as your Father in heaven is holy. Be perfect as He is perfect." We can't do it, but the power of the Holy Ghost living within us can.

The correction of this error in Church doctrine is the way the Church can align itself again with the Word of God. It is the revitalization of sanctification and holiness that the Church needs. When she rises up from the ashes of Laodicea (pitiful excuse used by today's Church) and takes her rightful place next to the Lord of Glory as the bride, dressed in robes of righteousness, shining and glorious without spot or wrinkle, then the world will be in awe of us and in awe of Him who commissions us (see Ephesians 5; Hebrews 12; Revelation 19). Then we will see His power unleashed upon the earth, for we will have come in line with His sovereignty.

The Church in Peril

Grace without Accountability

First Timothy 4:1–2: A false church arises in prominence during this period. Or, it may be more precise to say a false doctrine at the helm of some traditional churches. This doctrine strips Christ of His deity and denies the need for true repentance. It is devoid of accountability and responsibility for one's actions. It is a doctrine of grace without accountability. It teaches: "All you have to do is accept Jesus, it doesn't matter how you live." It is a damnable doctrine that has been funneled throughout the halls of justice, ascending to the pinnacle of government, leaving the residue in the elementary schools.

A Doctrinal Issue

True repentance, God-style, means, "to change our mind." It doesn't mean that you're perfect but that you've made up your mind not to do certain things and you don't do them. It is not a writ, or permission slip, to keep on sinning. The apostle Paul dealt with this and he said, "God forbid" that we should keep on sinning. The Lord Jesus by example demonstrated what was meant by true repentance.

In the Gospel of John, chapter eight, a woman who is caught in adultery was brought before Jesus by the Pharisees to be stoned. Jesus, after stooping down and writing in the sand, gave the unforgotten verdict: "Let he who is without sin cast the first stone."

As they all left one by one from the eldest to the youngest, He asked the woman for her accusers and if there was any man to condemn her. She acknowledges that she has no accusers. Jesus then sets precedent for all time and eternity. He says, "Neither do I condemn thee: Go and sin no more" (John 8: 1-11). Better translated, "Leave your life of sin."

Divine forgiveness is what everyone latches onto when they read this and they ignore the admonition and command "to go and sin no more." The directive the Lord is giving is to "leave your life of sin." The evidence of true repentance is the crucifixion of the sin nature. Nowhere does the Lord issue a license to sin, as is commonplace in our present day churches. It does not mean that we can't fail or make a mistake. But the lifestyle of sin must be "forsaken." This woman could not continue in adultery and maintain her status as a saint. The Bible forbids such. All unbelievers, adulterers, whoremongers, and those living a lie and making lies will burn in the lake of fire. The Bible is clear: See 1 Corinthians 6:9–11; Revelation 21:8; and Hebrews 13:4. The Bible has a word for those who engage in a lifestyle of sin after receiving salvation; it is called backsliding. This is what King David did when he committed adultery and murder, and there were some hefty consequences. Yet God is merciful and just to forgive us our sins and cleanse us from all unrighteousness. And when God forgives, He doesn't remember anymore. We may remember, but He doesn't.

A minister I knew commented about a famous TV evangelist who had fallen from grace when he said: "God will forgive him, but the people never will." Hence, the hypocrisy of the crowd. Those who truly know the Lord can only do as He did. Note: We are talking about forgiveness, not consequences. King David suffered consequences but received total forgiveness. We as believers have only one resolve when others ask for mercy: "Upon the grace of God I stand, I can do no other." (Speaking of falling away, if you want to know what is happening in the Church, this is it. "Except there be a falling away first, the Messiah can not come" [2 Thessalonians 2:3].)

Jesus did not preach a grace devoid of consequences as you hear from most pulpits. He did preach something new to the Pharisees. It was called grace. It is matchless and immeasurable, but it does not negate the standard "holiness" even if we spend our lives trying to walk in it. Be perfect as your Father in heaven is perfect. Be holy. It is what God has called us to do. If we mess up, His grace is the safety net. But, rest assured, your Bible would fall apart without consequences. If our society tried to run itself without a standard for law and order, we would have anarchy. And we ministers, even though we're blamed and imperfect, should bear the burden of the perfect and holy standard. God's holiness remains intact; he's not going to change. It is the grace of the Almighty God through the sacrifice of Christ that brings us up to the standard, and the power of the Holy Ghost, the Holy Spirit, dwelling in us that constrains us to the standard. It is grace and not works that saves us, but the evidence of that grace is the works that follow our conversion. That is why the Lord said, "A good tree brings forth good fruit and an evil tree brings forth evil fruit" (Matthew 7:15–20). Jesus advises us to look at the fruit, for by the fruit—deeds, or actions—you will know those of God. For those still not convinced that this is so, note that there are two books in Heaven, the Lamb's Book of Life and a book of deeds (Revelation 20:12–15). The Scripture mentions that all were judged according to their works. This is New Testament theology for us. The second chapter of Romans is the only means for judging those who have never heard the gospel (Romans 2:11).

Man's Problem

Man's problem is one of justification. He always seeks to justify himself and his actions, but before God we stand naked. There is no cloak, or covering, for our sins. Nothing we can say can dress it up. This was the dilemma of our American president and of King David in the Old Testament. There must be a way to cover up this sin—to dress it up so it doesn't look so bad, but sin is ugly. You can't dress it up. Against God's holiness, it's horrific. The only cloak, or covering, that we have for our sins is the mercy of God via the shed blood of Christ and our confession of helplessness before its evil blight. We throw ourselves upon the mercy of the Savior and accept whatever consequences

He chooses to level—never neglecting the fact that His standards and statutes are true and His way is sure; it is we who have missed the mark. There is nothing wrong with God or His holy Word. The fault lies in us. A.W. Tozer warned the evangelical church that it was becoming liberal, that this grace without accountability was not the gospel of the kingdom, as Paul scolded the Corinthian Church.

In 1 Corinthians 6:9–11, the apostle Paul was cautioning the Corinthian church, which believed it could inherit the kingdom and still engage in fornication and other sexual immorality. Paul was clear that this is the way we are but could not be the way we are to live in the kingdom of God.

John the Revelator tells us in Revelation 21:27 that nothing unclean will enter God's holy city, only those whose names are written in the Lamb's Book of Life, having all their sins and debts cancelled by the blood of Christ.

This by no means is an edict, negating all accountability after conversion. Again, the commandments of God are elevated in Revelation 22:14, "Blessed are they that do his commandments, that they may have right to the tree of life, and may enter in through the gates into the city." God has a holy standard. It is fulfilled in two mandates: "Love the Lord your God with all your mind, heart, and strength," and "Love your neighbor as yourself" (Matthew 22:34–40). *Any lack of love violates God's highest commandment and must be dealt with swiftly in the heart of the believer. God's love is sovereign evidence of true conversion.* Hence, Christ's statement, "They will know you are Christians by your love."

The Falling Away

The church has suffered a great falling away as was predicted in 2 Thessalonians 2:3: "Let no man deceive you by any means: for that day shall not come, except there come a falling away first, and that man of sin be revealed, the son of perdition."

The word for "falling away" is "apostasy" in the Greek! "Apostasy" here speaks of an abandonment of what one has formerly professed. When I was younger, everyone seemed to know what was right and what was wrong. Never have I seen a greater departure from what is true. Truth has been redefined as relative; it is whatever one believes. No wonder our children are so confused. *Listen, saints, believers, and nonbelievers: children need standards.* They need guidance through life. If we don't provide them with standards, some of the most heinous of crimes concocted will be committed by this generation. "If all truth is relative, then it doesn't matter what I do." This is the message being sent to the children. We know that according to the Bible all truth is absolute. God is absolutely right and man is absolutely wrong if he deviates from God's truth. Jesus said, "Know the truth and the truth shall make you free" (John 8:32).

Ministers in Ministry

This brings me to some ministerial house-cleaning. I will start with the positive. Some of the warmest, loving, and most genuine people I have ever met were pastors. Pastor Benjamin Garrison stands out as one of those pastors. His church was in one of the roughest sections of New York. At times, people were literally dodging bullets around New Year's or during a bad drug deal. The congregation had a lot of children from broken homes like mine before my father came back to Christ. Pastor Garrison became our "father." Many of the ladies came from dysfunctional marriages or divorce or fell into the unwed-mother syndrome. Pastor Garrison became everybody's father and to the older women their closest brother. He was such a godly man of prayer that when he spoke to you no matter what you were going through it stopped and the peace of God took over your being. He was also a sound doctrinal teacher of the Word of God. He refused to deviate from the text of the Holy Bible. He would say, "If it is not in the Word, throw it out." Old Brother Marshall, my Bible professor, would say, "If this isn't it, I'm holding onto this till it comes; I've found no better." Old Brother Marshall would also say he'd listen to a monkey if he were preaching the truth. We would all laugh.

Another pastor whom I cannot neglect to mention is Reverend Ronald J. Fowler, affectionately called "Pastor," of Akron, Ohio. Pastor Fowler has got to be one of the kindest people on earth. With my schedule, I may only see him once a year, but he greets me always as if we had just had a marvelous dinner the night before and he just wanted to thank me again for coming.

Having attended Catholic schools because the public schools in Cleveland were so horrible at the time, I must mention two priests: Reverend Francis P. Walsh and Reverend Thomas J. O'Malley. Father Walsh was also a man of prayer and incredibly kind. Once I needed a letter of reference, and a not-so-kind priest took it upon himself to write the letter. I was so distraught upon reading it that I took it to Father Walsh, the senior pastor. He read it, looked at me, and tore the letter to shreds before my eyes. He took out his pen and the church letterhead and wrote me one of the most beautiful letters that I had ever seen. I took it and sailed into the National Honor Society and Distinguished American High School Students. (Note: I did have the grades—just needed a kind reference).

Another benefactor whom I cannot fail to mention is Reverend Thomas J. O'Malley of John Carroll University. Father O'Malley is probably one of the most gifted priests I have ever encountered. As president of the university, he was very busy but always took the time to find out how I was doing when he saw me. In my junior year, the school raised tuition and I had run out of money. I went to him with a $1,000 bill and said that I didn't know what to do. He took the bill from me and told me, "Don't worry about it," and continued to chat with me about my classes. The next thing I knew I was issued an additional $1,000 scholarship from the university, which continued until I graduated.

On the other hand, some of the meanest, most self-centered, and egotistical individuals that I have ever met were pastors. These individuals were usually trying to build their own kingdom. Their names were everywhere. If I weren't grounded in the faith and the Word of God, I might have left the church forever after my encounters with some of them. They care more about programs and their policies than people and have left a lot of casualties along the way. If you have ever been hurt by one of them, there are enough good pastors to make up—just find the good ones.

CHAPTER 6

THE STATE OF THE UNION

As polarized as this country is politically, this is not a partisan issue. It is neither a Democratic nor Republican issue. This is a practical issue. No nation's treasury can withstand spending all its resources on war. The costliness of war brought down the French Empire, the Russian Empire, and the British Empire. It was the economic catalyst for their demise. (Go back to your history books and read it for yourself.) It was war that forced each of the kings and the British government to drain their nations' treasuries.

Prophetically, long before the 2004 election, I heard: "We began with George 'W' and we are going to end with George 'W.'" I do not know what that means. If it means the end of an era or what—I cannot speculate. (Those understanding prophecy know that it comes, "line upon line, precept upon precept, here a little, there a little" [Isaiah 28:9–11]). President George W. Bush well knows that there has not been a president named "George" since our first—George Washington—and later his father, Daddy Bush.

Regarding strategy, the president is surrounded by some brilliant political strategists. No president has ever held the White House by saying that he was "pro-choice." Since the issue evolved, Jimmy Carter—a Sunday school teacher—was pro-life. Ronald Reagan was absolutely pro-life. Daddy Bush was pro-life. When Bill Clinton was asked, he said that he was "pro-life but for a woman's right to choose." And George W. Bush is definitely pro-life. In 2004, the White House was John Kerry's to lose—he did not carry one Southern state. He did not understand the culture of the South (the Bible Belt) and the Midwest. To his credit, and that of John Edwards, they did bring up the concern for national health care for millions of Americans and the necessity of improving diplomatic relations with our allies. This analysis is from the heart of a true moderate.

Have the Terrorists Won?

We are spending billions on anti-terrorism, throwing money at a problem without assessing the need. On 9/11, or September 11, 2001, we had two (2) problems:

1. *Our airline security was in the hands of a private industry whose bottom line was the almighty "buck." Obviously, you get what you pay for. Poorly paid employees were in charge of our air security, and possession of box cutters—illegal in most Third World nations—was legal in American air travel.*

2. *We let anybody and everybody into our country—being ignorant of the fact that not everybody loved us or our way of life, ignorant of the fact that there were people insane with jealousy at our prosperity and power that wanted to strike at us just because we are Americans. Again, we had two problems.*

Today, fear is running our country, and overboard and overkill are in the driver's seat. We had two internal problems on 9/11 that needed to be fixed; however, presently, we are surrendering our freedom in the name of security. We are legislating away our freedoms in the name of fear. Out of fear, we are giving up our right to move freely, communicate freely, and to trade and transact business freely. Is this not what they (the terrorists) wanted—to bankrupt us out of fear? To have us fight enemies everywhere and to spread our resources so thin as to render us ineffective as a superpower? To so entangle us in the affairs of this world that it would be impossible for us to extricate ourselves? To violate the one tenet, or principle, that the first "George," George Washington, had warned us to stay clear of: "the entanglement in foreign affairs"?

Was it not this entanglement that led us into Vietnam? In our War against Terrorism, how will we know we've won? Where is the exit? If we must defend our allies or ourselves, we must not go it alone—only in extreme cases of self-defense (i.e. Afghanistan). We must build an international coalition and allow the rest of the concerned world to shoulder the burden.

Now back to our original premise: "Have the terrorists won?" If the American people surrender their freedoms to anyone for any reason, then the terrorists have won. *God forbid!*

In conclusion, it is only fitting to close with Washington's farewell address, which is surreal and haunting given our present circumstance:

The nation which indulges toward another an habitual hatred or an habitual fondness is in some degree a slave. It is a slave to its animosity or to its affection, either of which is sufficient to lead it astray from its duty and its interests.

—Boller, p. 89

Again, Washington's Farewell admonishes:

It is our true policy to steer clear of permanent alliances with any portion of the foreign world, so far, I mean as we are now at liberty to do it....Taking care always to keep ourselves by suitable establishments on a respectable defensive posture, we may safely trust to temporary alliances for extraordinary emergencies....Harmony, liberal intercourse with all nations are recommended by policy, humanity, and interest. But even our commercial policy should hold an equal and impartial hand, neither seeking nor granting exclusive favors or preferences.

—Boller, p. 90

We have strayed so far from our founding father's admonition; we are entangled everywhere. We have indulged in habitual hatred toward communist states, which has dragged us into numerous wars and conflicts and which

now seem pointless, seeing that we now communicate and trade with most of these nations.
Under Ronald Reagan, we found a more excellent way of wooing them with our way of life and
letting them choose—rather than bullying them
and propping up puppet governments to do what
we want, which only further entangles us with
malice. (Note: Even former Russian President
Gorbachev attended Mr. Reagan's funeral, revealing the high regard of his more excellent way.)
As much as it is possible with the US, our goal
should be trade and not war. Trade bolsters a
nation's economy and employs its people—wars
deplete its treasury and its people.

On 9/11

We answered the president's call for war
because September 11, 2001, was a day of terror, but it was not because of weapons of mass
destruction. Nine-eleven occurred because of our
neglect to secure our own air space. It was "our
planes" that were turned into bombs. Again, it
was because we left the security of our air space
to private industry and not to our national government where it belonged. We are allowing fear
rather than reason to dictate policy. Our leaders must think rationally about all that we are
doing in the name of security. We have sought

to fix our air security problem, but we have not thought about how our actions to change a regime or topple a government may encourage other nations to do the same with those nations that they have trouble with. We lead by example. Should China, Russia, and North Korea seek to rid themselves of potential hostile nations, will we support them?

Oil Prophecy

The only logical reason for taking out Saddam Hussein is to protect Israel and American interests in the Middle East, namely oil. The world's economy and stability revolves around oil. As is prophesied, "A penny of wheat for a measure of barley. Two pennies of wheat for a measure of barley. Touch not the oil or the wine" (Revelation 6:6). Oil and wine will never lose its value, even near the end of time. Stabilizing oil prices is a key to stabilizing industrial world economies.

On the Wisdom of War

> Wisdom is better than weapons of war...
> —Ecc. 9:18

As long as your enemies are inferior to you in skill, strategy, and ability, and you maintain your position of strength (i.e., Third-World nations), the "might makes right" proposition can prevail, or the most powerful nation can dictate all negotiating terms. However, maneuvering from a position of strength and superiority is a dangerous proposition against allies who have been waging war for centuries and whose strategic diplomatic ability and combined strength are no match for a lone-ranger cowboy. George Washington had this understanding with regard to Europe. Remember: "The beginning of wisdom is fear of the Lord" (Proverbs 1:7). Even the Lord knew that to rule from a position of fear forever is failure (i.e., the Old Testament theology of law alone gave way to the New Testament theology of grace and truth [John 1:17]). The better way—the more excellent way—is to make all fall in love with you (your prosperity, your freedom, and your peace); hence, the Lord Jesus' example.

On Pestilence, or Disease

Matthew 24:7 includes pestilence, or disease, as the beginning of sorrows. Just when we thought that we had at least conquered, educated about, or limited the transmission of AIDS, here comes SARS (Severe Acute Respiratory Syndrome). AIDS has killed millions of people and counting, not to mention the residue of HIV, which had its rapid rise among teenagers and homosexuals and reached epidemic proportions in Africa and Asia.

SARS had been multiplying exponentially, and what is so frightening is that it appears to be like the flu and is transmitted by air. Most importantly, it has proven to be deadly and is without a cure. We know it has its origin in China and has at one point shut down air travel, unless absolutely necessary, to Hong Kong, China, and even Toronto. So far, SARS has claimed hundreds of lives.

Pestilence, or disease, is nothing new. In the Bible, the dreaded disease was leprosy, the rotting away of the appendages (fingers, toes, noses, etc.) before death. In the Middle Ages, it was the Bubonic plague, which wiped out a third of the population of Europe.

Today, devious nations play around with these diseases and plot and scheme with biochemical warfare. In the age of suicide bombers, who have no regard for their own lives, much less the lives of others, we see we are on the precipices of disaster. It is only a matter of time before a suicide bomber uses biochemical warfare to make a statement. Lord Jesus, spare Your people. Father God, protect us.

The Return of Christ

Matthew 24:34 says, "And this generation shall not pass until all these things be fulfilled." Never before has the stage been so set for the return of Christ:

1. *Once again, Israel has become a nation, which is crucial to end-time prophecy (Jeremiah 33:20–26, Daniel 9:24–27). In 1948, Israel was granted nation status.*

2. *Jerusalem is no longer under the control of the Gentiles ("And Jerusalem shall be trodden down of the Gentiles until the time of the Gentiles be fulfilled" [Luke 21:24].) In 1967, control of Jerusalem reverted to the Jews.*

3. *The signs of the times are here: progressive and destructive wars, famines, pestilence, and earthquakes till the end. "For nation shall rise against nation, and kingdom against kingdom: and there shall be famines, and pestilence, and earthquakes in divers or various places. All these are the beginning of sorrows....And this gospel of the kingdom shall be preached in all the world for a witness unto all nations; and then shall the end come" (Matthew 24:7–8, 14). "Now learn a par-*

able of the fig tree; When his branch is yet tender, and putteth forth leaves, you know that summer is near; so likewise, when you shall see all these things, know that it is near, even at the doors. Verily, I say unto you, This generation shall not pass, till all these things be fulfilled" (Matthew 24:32–34). *This generation has lived through two world wars.*

4. *The birth of nuclear warfare gives man the capacity to wipe out his race and all life forms. "And this shall be the plague wherewith the* LORD *will smite all the people that have fought against Jerusalem; Their flesh shall consume away while they stand upon their feet, and their eyes shall consume away in their holes, and their tongue shall consume away in their mouth"* (Zechariah 14:12). *("But the day of the Lord will come as a thief in the night; in the which the heavens shall pass away with a great noise, and the elements shall melt with fervent heat, the earth also and the works that are therein shall be burned up"* [2 Peter 3:10].) *Never before has man possessed the arsenals to destroy the world and himself, and never before has the possibility of such*

force falling into the hands of those who would use it been so probable.

5. *The most profitable industries are those that have to do with knowledge or the transfer of information (i.e., the computer, the telephone, education, and TV). ("But thou, O Daniel, shut up the words, and seal the book, even to the time of the end: many shall run to and fro, and knowledge shall be increased" [Daniel 12:4].) We see people running all over the world to get the latest story, and we are immersed in the greatest information craze ever.*

6. *Israel has reached its fiftieth anniversary as a nation (1948–1998). We are this generation of apocalyptic fulfillment ("This generation shall not pass until all these things be fulfilled" [Matthew 24:34]).*

7. *The whole world will see the two witnesses of God. ("And they of the people and kindreds and tongues and nations shall see their dead bodies three days and an half, and shall not suffer their bodies to be put in graves. . . . And after three days and an half the spirit of life from God entered into them, and they stood upon their feet; and great fear fell upon*

them which saw them" [Revelation 11:9, 11].) This media age and international television makes this possible.

8. *The Rapture of the Church, "Harpazo," or "the great catching away" has been the hope of all for centuries who love His appearing. ("For the Lord himself shall descend from heaven with a shout, with the voice of the archangel, and with the trump of God: and the dead in Christ shall rise first: then we which are alive and remain shall be caught up together with them in the clouds, to meet the Lord in the air: and so shall we ever be with the Lord. Wherefore comfort one another with these words" [1 Thessalonians 4:16–18].) ("Behold, I show you a mystery; we shall not all sleep, but we shall all be changed, in a moment, in the twinkling of an eye, at the last trump: for the trumpet shall sound, and the dead shall be raised incorruptible, and we shall be changed. For this corruptible must put on incorruption, and this mortal must put on immortality" [1 Corinthians 15:51–53].) Hey, if it could be completely understood, it wouldn't be a mystery.*

CHAPTER 7

THE DAVIDIC COVENANT IN ITS MODERN DAY FULFILLMENT OF THE UNITED STATES AND BRITAIN

The purpose here is three-fold: first, to establish that God made a covenant with David; second, to establish that this covenant is lasting and temporal in its fulfillment and has prophetic ramifications for the United States and Britain; and finally, to declare that Jesus Christ is the everlasting fulfillment of the Davidic Covenant to the letter.

First, we must begin with a little background on David. David was the youngest of the sons of Jesse of the tribe of Judah. He was a shepherd boy, one of the humblest tasks of an Israelite. David was anointed king above all his brothers by the most esteemed prophet, Samuel. The king at the time, Saul, chased David for twenty years, trying to kill him out of jealousy. This greatly humbled the man of God; yet, when he had opportunity to kill the king, David proved himself righteous and cried out with holy reverence, "Touch not God's anointed and do his prophets no harm." In return, God wiped out all of David's enemies and established him as king (1 Samuel 16–2 Samuel 5). (Note: Humility was also a characteristic of Moses, the standard bearer of the Old Covenant in Numbers 11. It is very important to God.)

Even in failure, David behaved himself justly, humbling himself under the judgments of God, allowing his own son to drive him out of the kingdom. However, David remained the "man after God's own heart." His indiscretion is only mentioned once in the history of Israel. His character so pleased God that God vowed to establish an everlasting covenant with the House of David that could not be revoked even upon the failure of some of Judah's future kings (2 Samuel 7:12–17) (Conner and Malmin, p. 63). This brings us to a discussion of the covenant and David's arrival at God's promises.

After conquering all of his enemies and bringing the Ark of the Covenant, God's Mercy Seat, back into the kingdom, David was deeply disturbed that he was living in a palatial paradise while God's throne, the Ark of the Covenant, was housed in a barn. This thing upset David so that he called Nathan the prophet and told him that he wanted to build a house for the Ark of God. In his wildest dreams, David could never have anticipated God's response:

And it came to pass that night that the word of the LORD came unto Nathan saying, "Now, therefore so shalt thou say unto my servant David, 'Thus saith the LORD of hosts, "I took thee from the sheepcote, from following the sheep, to be ruler over my people over Israel: And I was with thee whithersoever thou wentest, and have cut off all thine enemies out of thy sight, and have made thee a great name like unto the name of great men that are in the earth… And when thy days be fulfilled, and thou shalt sleep with thy fathers, I will set up thy seed after thee, which shall proceed out of thy bowels, and I will establish his kingdom forever. I will be his father, and he shall be my son. If he commit iniquity, I will chasten him with the rod of men, and with the stripes of the children of men: But my mercy shall not depart away from him, as I took it from Saul, whom I put away before thee. And thine house and thy kingdom shall be established forever before thee; thy throne shall be established forever."'"

—2 Sam. 7:8–9, 12–17

Note the language of this covenant. This is a "*diatheke*" covenant, or a one-party performance contract. Only God can perform this contract. He is the only one that has the power to establish the throne of David forever (2 Samuel 7:12–13). There is nothing that David can do to compensate for God's offer. God makes no special request of David in this covenant. David can rest in the fact that God said He would perform it and it shall come to pass. Now this covenant raises some historical questions that cannot go unanswered if we are to take God at His Word.

Is This Covenant Unconditional?

According to the words of the Lord, this covenant is unconditional and irrevocable. God makes no mistake by even giving an example of the conditions. He says that if a son or heir of David should, while he was reigning,

"commit iniquity, I will chasten him with the rod of men, and with the stripes of the children of men: But my mercy shall not depart away from him, as I took it from Saul, whom I put away before thee. And thy house and thy kingdom shall be established forever before thee: thy throne shall be established forever."

—2 Sam. 7:14–16

So this covenant is binding irrespective of generational circumstances or moral failure.

Now, some theologians say that the covenant is conditional in that in order for the successors of David to be blessed, they had to walk uprightly (Tenney, p. 40). However, this condition has to do with blessing, and it does nothing to negate the existence and longevity of David's throne (Unger, p. 465). God has mandated that the throne would continue irrespective of moral failure. "This promise finds its fulfillment in the unbroken dynasty of Davidic kings from Solomon to Zedekiah in the promised land" (Conner and Malmin, p. 61).

The next question poses a theological and historical dilemma for those who maintain that Christ is the natural fulfillment of the Davidic Covenant and who dig no further: *How could the throne that was promised to be fulfilled forever be vacant for six centuries?* (Conner and Malmin, p. 62).

From the time of Judah's last king, Zedekiah, to the spiritual fulfillment in Christ, there has lapsed six centuries. Some theologians maintain that "[t]he natural and national fulfillment from the time of Zedekiah [until Christ] was unneeded and irrelevant because of the spiritual fulfillment that came in Christ six centuries later (Luke 1:30–33; Acts 2:29–36)" (Conner and Malmin, p. 62).

Theologians who reject this view maintain that

> though this theory accurately sees the ultimate fulfillment of the seed of David in Christ, it belittles and undermines God's carefulness to watch over His Covenant word in an apparent "breach of promise."
>
> —Ps. 89:34–38, 49
> —Conner and Malmin, p. 62–63

God would not have said forever if He did not mean forever. A six-century lapse in time interferes with the covenant promise of "forever." One of the immutable things about God's character is: "He cannot lie." He is not a man that he should lie or change His mind, Hallelujah! (Hebrews 6:16–18). If God says forever, it is forever.

We can be sure of this: God kept His Word. The throne could not be vacant for six centuries and God kept His promise. In fact, the fulfillment of this promise has great ramifications for the world today (see below), and for surety, it completes the prophecy of the 144-year-old patriarch, Israel, as he leaned upon his staff.

The Covenants, by Kevin Conner and Ken Malmin, was the final confirmation I needed that the following theory is more than a theory but the historical reality that confirms the Word of God and upholds the Promise Keeper's—Yahweh's, the Lord Jehovah's—strict attention to detail, neglecting not a jot or tittle to perform His Word (see Matthew 5:18). Hallelujah!

The Prophet Jeremiah

Throughout time, God has used history to confirm the Bible of which one third is history. The most extensive study and reparation of this breach in prophecy is *The United States and Britain in Prophecy*, written by the former editor and founder of the Ambassador College, Herbert W. Armstrong.

First, let us deal with the six-century gap. The prophet at the time was the prophet Jeremiah; he was the presiding prophet during the reign of Zedekiah. The nation of Israel and Judah (under Zedekiah) had both gone astray and become apostate. The Lord was angry and was determined to remove Judah as He removed Israel (2 Kings 23:27) (Armstrong, p. 74). However, there was one hurdle: His covenant with David.

Jeremiah is given a mysterious commission from the Lord:

> "See, I have this day set thee over the nations and over the kingdoms, to root out, and to pull down, and to destroy, and to throw down, to build and to plant."
>
> —Jer. 1:10

Secular history maintains that after Zedekiah's eyes were gouged out and his sons murdered, the prophet Jeremiah took a daughter of Zedekiah to marry a prince of the House of Israel in the British Isles in order to preserve the Davidic throne. "This made a lineage of the kings of Ireland, Scotland and England and the ongoing fulfillment of the natural and earthly throne of David" (Genesis 38; Jeremiah 41:10, 43:6, 44:14, 15:11, 33:17, 24–26) (Conner and Malmin, p. 63; Armstrong, pp. 99–100).

Though secular history is not inspired or infallible as Bible history is, it does hold clues that should be considered when interpreting biblical prophecy. British history includes such clues as the tomb of Jeremiah, a scribe named

Baruch, a king's daughter, a stone called "Jacob's Stone," where British kings are anointed, and a genealogy tracing British kings back to David. These clues are either fraudulent or are evidence for the best known explanation of the natural fulfillment of the Davidic Covenant, which is, that the kings of Ireland, Scotland, and England have perpetuated the dynasty of David (Conner and Malmin, p. 63).

What ramifications does this have on today's prophecy concerning Britain and the United States, and how does this tie into the patriarch's, Israel's, prophecy concerning Ephraim and Manasseh?

The prophet Jeremiah records the temporal continuity of the throne of David:

> And the word of the LORD came unto Jeremiah, saying, "Thus saith the LORD: 'If ye can break my covenant of the day and my covenant of the night, and that there should not be day and night in their season; Then may also my covenant be broken with David my servant, that he should not have a son to reign upon his throne; and with the Levites the priest, my ministers. As the host of heaven cannot be numbered, neither the sand of the sea measured; so will I multiply the seed of David my servant and the Levites that minister unto me.'"

Moreover, the word of the LORD came to Jeremiah, saying, "Considerest thou not what his people have spoken, saying, 'The two families which the LORD hath chosen, he hath even cast them off?' Thus they have despised my people, that they should be no more a nation before them.'" Thus saith, the LORD: If my covenant be not with day and night and if I have not appointed the ordinances of heaven and earth; Then will I cast away the seed to be rulers over the seed of Abraham, Issac, and Jacob: for I will cause their captivity to return, and have mercy on them."

—Jer. 33:19–26

Digging a little deeper, we uncover in history some of the most fascinating and illuminating prophetic pieces of the Abrahamic and Davidic Covenants. As old Jacob (Israel) extended his hands to bless the sons of Joseph and confer the birthright blessing, he crossed his hands. Joseph sought to stop him, but Israel refused, maintaining that the younger one, Ephraim, will be greater than the older one, Manasseh. The older one will be great, but the younger one will become a multitude of nations (Genesis 48:13–20). Here, Jacob was referring to the prophecy that he received at Bethel where God changed his name from Jacob to Israel and told him that "a nation and a company of nations shall be of thee, and kings shall come out of thy loins" (Genesis 35:10–11).

Many theologians and historians have interpreted *the nation to be Great Britain and the company of nations to be America* and the kings to be *the House of David* transplanted in *the royal house of London* (Conner and Malmin, p. 32–33, 63; Armstrong, p. 105–106).

In the natural, we know that "the sun never set on the British Empire" at the height of her power. It was Great Britain that sanctioned the establishment of the nation of Israel in 1948 (Palmer and Colton, pp. 869–870). It was Queen Victoria who knighted Sir Rothchild, the financier, to finance the Zionists. It was Great Britain that refused the rule of Rome over the Church and made the monarch head of church and state, paving the way for individual worship toward God. It was King James that sanctioned the printing of the English Bible, the most original and widely read English document in modern times. This is the only monarchy protected by guards without weapons.

As Britain declined in status after World Wars I and II, America rose, representing a melting pot of nations, or "a company of nations." It is believed that, in opening her doors to the world,

America has captured the lost House of Israel (Conner and Malmin, pp. 32–33). Now the following parallels are astounding; either they are true or the most incredible coincidences in all of modern history:

1. *Israel had thirteen tribes (twelve tribes plus Levi); America had thirteen colonies upon inception.*

2. *Ephraim/Israel split with the House of Judah over being overly taxed by the king (1 Kings 12:1–24); America split with Great Britain over being overly taxed by King George.*

3. *As Great Britain was responsible for establishing Israel, America has sought to ensure her existence, being her most formidable ally.*

4. *Ephraim is to be "a multitude of nations;" America's greatest symbol is Lady Liberty who welcomes all to her doors of which America has become a "melting pot of nations."*

5. *The ties between America and Great Britain are outstanding. We've been on the same side in every world war. Also, there is the American fascination with the royal family. We attend their weddings*

and mourn at their funerals. (The most recent example of this was the marriage and death of Princess Diana.)

Jesus, Son of David

Finally, the most uncontested truth among Christian scholars is that Jesus is the fulfillment of the Davidic Covenant.

> It is notable that all the gospel writers seek to make clear the relation between the Lord Jesus and David. With great frequency Matthew and the other writers note this relationship by the term "the son of David" which is applied to Jesus....The great thesis of the gospels is that Jesus fulfills exactly all of the conditions and promises of God's covenant with David, that a seed should never fail on his throne. Jesus is the seed of David and the eternal King whom God had promised (Matthew 1:1; 9:27; 12:23; Mark 10:48; 12:35; Luke 18:38–39, 20:41).
>
> —Tenney, p. 42

For someone who has never written anything, *the Lord Jesus has had more books written about Him than any other person in history*, and the volumes cannot contain the books concerning His rule from Heaven. He indeed is:

Wonderful Counselor, Mighty God, Everlasting
Father, Prince of Peace, Beloved Savior, Justi-
fier, Sanctifier, Friend of Man, Lover of Mankind,
Good Shepherd from on High, Masterful Admin-
istrator, etc., etc., etc. Again, the volumes cannot
contain the books.

BIBLIOGRAPHY

Armstrong, Herbert W. *The United States and Britain in Prophecy.* USA: Worldwide Church of God 1980.

Boller, Paul F. and Ronald Story. *A More Perfect Union: Documents in US History.* Volume I. Boston, Massachusetts: Houghton Mifflin Company, 1984.

Breese, Dave. *Europe and the Prince That Shall Come.* Hillsboro, Kansas: Christian Destiny, Inc., 1989.

Conner, Kevin and Ken Malmin. *The Covenants.* Portland, Oregon: Bible Temple Publishing, 1983.

McDow, Malcom and Alvin L. Reid. *Firefall: How God Has Shaped History Through Revivals*. Nashville, Tennessee: Broadman & Holman Publishers, 1997.

Palmer, RR. and Joel Coltan. *A History of the Modern World Since 1815*. New York, New York: Alfred A. Knopf, Inc., 1978.

Pentecost, Dwight. *Things To Come*. Grand Rapids, Michigan: Zondervan Publishing House, 1958.

Pfeiffer, Charles F. and Everett F. Harrison. *The Wycliffe Bible Commentary*. Chicago, Illinois: Moody Press, 1962.

Scofield, C.I. *The Scofield Study Bible*. New York, New York: Oxford University Press, 1909.

Strong, James. *Strong's Exhaustive Concordance of the Bible*. McLean, Virginia: McDonald Publishing Co., 1986.

Tenney, Merrill C. *New Testament Survey*. Leicester, England: Intervarsity Press, 1985.

Vine, W.E., Merrill F. Unger and William White Jr. *Expository Dictionary of Old and New Testament Words*. Nashville, Tennessee: Thomas Nelson, Inc., 1985.

Van Impe, Jack. *The 80's, the Antichrist and Your Startling Future*. USA: Jack Van Impe Ministries, 1982.

To order additional copies of

BEYOND ALL CONTROVERSY

Have your credit card ready and call:

1-877-421-READ (7323)

or please visit our web site at
www.pleasantword.com

Also available at:
www.amazon.com
and
www.barnesandnoble.com

Printed in the United States
148557LV00001B/27/A

9 781414 104294